"A child with a vision is discovering his talent—but does he have to be absolutely insane to follow his gift? Dean Kostos's memoir, *The Boy Who Listened to Paintings*, tells the incredible story of a young, middle-class, gay boy of Greek heritage who catches his beloved, imaginative mother's 'crazy germs.' Ostracized in the wake of her breakdown, this son from a prominent family (his father is the town mayor) spends two years in a mental hospital. All alone, he has to reckon with his gun-toting brother, the fierce prejudices of mental health professionals, the intense bullying in schools, and the drug culture peer pressure in the 'Toot,' as he calls the hospital where he manages to survive. All that is thanks to a slow realization that art itself is health. Riveting—and outraging now—*The Boy Who Listened to Paintings* is a warmly brilliant memoir of adolescence and mental health to inspire all of us."

Molly Peacock, author of *Paradise, Piece by Piece*

"This harrowing account of a boy's (mis)treatment in a mental institution, where he narrowly missed becoming one more suicide statistic, offers much to ponder concerning highly topical issues like family dysfunction, bullying, homophobia, sexual harassment, and the failure of our society to support its young people. Tragedy here has a good outcome, though, when the victim finds his way out of the infernal maze with the assistance of art, Asian spirituality, and Christianity. Inevitably the memoir calls to mind the old narrative of Christ's harrowing of Hell, and we greet the escapee with sighs of relief and cheers for his will to regain his health and to transform suffering into a work of art."

Alfred Corn, author of *Contradictions* and *Unions*

PREVIOUS PRAISE FOR DEAN KOSTOS'S POETRY:

"The grace of Dean Kostos's texts (I would call it *unconscious* grace, for that is the adjective which permits all heaven as much as all hell to explode, to let fly) is the result of another effort, not even the effort to please, but merely—merely!—the will to tell the truth, *to tell what happened, what didn't.* .

Richard Howard

D0896857

Also by Dean Kostos

Poetry
Pierced by Night-Colored Threads
This Is Not a Skyscraper
(recipient of the Benjamin Saltman Award,
selected by Mark Doty)
Rivering
Last Supper of the Senses
The Sentence That Ends with a Comma
Celestial Rust

Play
Box-Triptych

Choral Text
Dialogue: Angel of Peace, Angel of War

Editor
*Pomegranate Seeds: An Anthology of Greek-American
Poetry*

Coeditor
Mama's Boy: Gay Men Write About Their Mothers

THE BOY WHO LISTENED TO PAINTINGS

Dean Kostos

SPUYTEN DUYVIL
NEW YORK CITY

ACKNOWLEDGMENTS

Excerpted portions of this memoir appeared in the following publications:

"The Clay Swan," *Mama's Boy: Gay Men Write about Their Mothers*
"Descending the Staircase," *New Madrid*
"Obeying the Doll God," *The Dos Passos Review*
"Gun World," *Memoir Journal*
"The Toot," *Salon Zine*
"Crazy-Germs," *Storyscape Journal*
"Vow," *Storyscape Journal*
"Cabal," *The Same*
"The Ban," *The Woven Tale Press*

I extend my deepest gratitude to the trustees at Yaddo, where I began this memoir. I can never adequately thank the following people who have read through various drafts of the manuscript and offered guidance: Constantine Contogenis, Richard Goodman, Penelope Karageorge, Benee Knauer, Fayre Makeig, Ernesto Mestre, Molly Peacock, Nicholas Samaras, Violet Turner, Bonnie Walker, and Michael T. Young.

Some of the scenes and situations were adjusted for dramatic purposes.
Many names have been changed.
I have not, however, changed Lenore's name.

Library of Congress Cataloging-in-Publication Data

Names: Kostos, Dean, author.
Title: The boy who listened to paintings / Dean Kostos.
Description: New York City : Spuyten Duyvil, 2019.
Identifiers: LCCN 2018053146 | ISBN 9781949966077
Subjects: LCSH: Kostos, Dean,--Mental health. | Mentally ill children--United
    States--Rehabilitation--Biography. | Mentally ill--Patients--United
    States--Biography. | Mentally ill parents--United States--Biography. |
    Mentally ill--Family relationships.
Classification: LCC RJ499 .K646 2019 | DDC 618.92/890092 [B] --dc23
LC record available at https://lccn.loc.gov/2018053146

Dedicated to Sofia Kostos, Zili Kraus,
Sarala Ruth Pinto, and Emily Williams

"The day the child realizes that all adults are imperfect,
he becomes an adolescent;
the day he forgives them, he becomes an adult;
the day he forgives himself, he becomes wise."
                    —Alden Nowlan

Contents

PROLOGUE

Distance widened between me and my parents, between me and the world. Clattering down a hall, we came to a door. My father rang the buzzer. A nurse let us in, the safety-glass door slamming behind us.

Recognizing the ward, my mother hissed, "Still the same." Her eyes were raw from crying. She pulled out a compact, dipped a pad in flesh-colored makeup to cover dark circles. Twisting a lipstick tube, she traced her mouth into a coral-red *no*.

A man appeared. "Kostos?" he asked. We nodded. He ushered Mom and Dad into a conference room. Their dazed reflections swam in the glass surface of the table. The administrator handed out forms. I stood by the open door as my parents turned page after page, scribbling their names, answering questions. They handed the papers to the man who discussed their responsibilities. I pretended not to listen, but curiosity won out. I slouched into the windowless room. My father said he and Mom would do anything to speed my recovery. She repeated, "Anything."

A scrim separated Dad from me—I didn't believe he wanted to help. And I couldn't look Mom in the eye. I knew I'd hurt her.

After hugs so tight I thought our bodies would burst, after kisses and suppressed tears, after my parents promised to visit—they shuffled out the door. I peered through its webbed pane. My mother, biting her lip, glanced back. My father pulled her forward.

Vents shushed. I was alone.

The word *committed* no longer referred to devotion to a task, hobby, or friend. Its new meaning ricocheted through my brain. No one knew, but at age fourteen, I had schemed to get myself admitted to The Institute of Pennsylvania Hospital: a loony bin, a nuthouse, an insane asylum.

Puffing on a menthol cigarette, an aide introduced herself and escorted me to my room. The hall reeked, a nostril-piercing stench. The aide said it was disinfectants, used to mop up blood from patients who'd "hurt themselves." I remembered that odor from seven years before. The past rose up around me: *Here I am—where Mom was committed when I was a kid.*

CHAPTER 1
ROCK GARDEN

When I was seven, I overheard my mother telling Dad he should hug me. His answer didn't come as a surprise: He said I sickened him. I never knew why, but he pulled away whenever I got near him. It made me feel dirty.

Maybe if I worked harder, he'd come around to liking me. I took out my penmanship homework and practiced. I wrote till my hand cramped up. But I kept on writing. It had to be perfect. The following day, I showed it to my teacher. She stuck a gold star on the top. I couldn't wait to go home and show Dad.

But I saw him before getting there. His face was gray, his hair black as his suit. Trudging the mile from school to home, I passed a black-and-white reelection poster of him, the mayor of our South Jersey town, Cinnaminson. I squinted at the towering photograph.

Coming to our house, I passed our rock garden. Tiger lilies like speckled flames. I cut a right onto the walkway. Our neighbor Zili waited by the front door. "Sweetheart, I have an important message for you and Phillip," she said, her Romanian accent curling his name.

"Isn't Mommy—"

"Let's wait for your brother." Zili and I sat on the ledge. She squeezed my hand, dry clay crusted on her nails. We finally spotted Phil.

"What's goin' on?" he said.

"I didn't want you boys coming home to an empty house."

"Where's Mom?" he asked.

"She's … not feeling so good." Zili invited us into her house, where her husband said hello and disappeared. I knew something was wrong and wanted to run but felt nauseous. I stood there staring at her paintings, prints, and sculptures—thinking back on the summer before.

She had transformed this rec room into a Parisian café, with "artistes" in berets. They performed for the audience. Instead of clapping, people snapped their fingers after every poem and song. I liked the laughing sound of their voices—like a wave I was riding. Zili had made a world where we could be anywhere, do anything.

Now that rec room was silent, all joy gone out. A whiff of buttered vegetables tugged me back to the present. Her husband padded into the room with a bowl of carrots and snow peas. Zili carried a platter of broiled meat. The steaks were shaped like South America. But I had no appetite.

"What's wrong with Mommy?" I asked.

"She's gone to a hospital to help her feel less sad," Zili said.

"They stick you in the hospital for being sad?" Phillip asked.

"A different kind of hospital," she said.

I guessed it was my fault, remembering when Mommy made me clean the house while Phil went out to play. I whined that it wasn't fair. I wished I could take back my angry words.

Then it hit me—maybe it was worse. Instead of saying what really happened, Zili and her husband had that embarrassed, too-polite look adults get when they're scared. Did Mommy die?

4

Once in the woods behind our house, I saw a trap bite clear through a muskrat's leg, its fur bright red. I tried to talk, but my mouth-trap wouldn't let words out. Consonants—*b*'s and *f*'s mostly—stuttered from my lips. Although I stammered at school, I didn't usually do so at home. Without realizing it, I bit the inside of my mouth, as if I were eating myself. It hurt, but I couldn't stop or get up. Even the pain didn't shake me. I stared into the blue-gray flicker of the TV.

Finally, the doorbell chimed. My father had come to bring Phillip and me home. Dad's black hair was oily, his face shiny, as if he'd been sweating. He wouldn't look me in the eye.

CHAPTER 2
IN THE TOOT

The Institute of Pennsylvania Hospital. Dad, Phil, and I visited Mommy there. During her month-and-a-half stay, we never missed a week. The first time, we waited in the lunchroom. A woman with messy hair approached me. I told her I was visiting my mother but couldn't pronounce the word "Insa-tute." The woman told me not to worry. Insiders called it the "Toot." Her nurse led her away.

At the end of the lunchroom, I found a newsstand and gift shop. Seeing my favorite candy—Rolo—I asked Dad for a nickel. He said, "What? You want to take away five of my friends? What a selfish boy." I said nothing more.

Finally, Mommy showed up: groggy, hair pulled back in a ponytail. The "sadness" floated in her eyes like something she couldn't blink away. She walked in a trance, and we followed her. We came to a lawn where patients and visitors played volleyball or talked in Adirondack chairs. Some people stared into space or argued with invisible enemies. But an amazing thing happened: Marching across the lawn, I made the patients' bad feelings disappear. Their eyes lit up as they greeted me, "Hello, little boy." I hoped I could make Mommy feel better, too.

We followed her below catalpa trees. Dad picked a flower, tucked it behind her ear, and whispered something. My parents dodged each other's eyes, heads almost touching. I didn't want them to know I was watching. I turned away and noticed a lady in an orange wig headed toward us. I thought she was a clown. Giving my brother and me sticks of chewing gum, she said, all in one big rush, "Hi my name's Peggy look I have chewing gum for you in all different flavors with funny striped colors I make bracelets with them I can make some for you would you wear them?" That colors and flavors went together made sense. It was a way of putting things in order, the way I collected leaves, ironed between waxed paper and labeled in my scrapbook: Hornbeam, Hawthorn, Winged Elm. I told the Clown Lady I liked her bracelets but said my friends wouldn't understand if I wore them. I promised to show her my scrapbook the following Saturday.

The next week, my stuttering got worse at school. When my teacher called on me to read, I pleaded with my eyes, *Don't make me do this.*

Her reply, "Dean, we don't have all day."

I couldn't get through one sentence without making a *wuh-wuh-wuh* sound. Some kids imitated me. Others erupted into laughter. I sat down, my face burning. But that didn't stop the teacher from calling on me again.

The following Saturday, instead of seeing the Clown Lady, we met with Mommy and her psychiatrist. He talked Dad into getting Phil and me to see psychologists. Telling my father I was too close to Mommy, the man arranged for me to see a male therapist. Self-conscious about my chewed nails, I noticed his perfect hands. He smiled and asked me to play with a doll family, whose rubber bodies caved in when I squeezed their hollow legs. Then I embarrassed myself by stuttering. He asked if I wanted to work with someone who could help me. I thanked him and went back to playing. He scribbled notes on a yellow pad.

Within days, he scheduled me to work with a speech therapist at school. Three times a week, I sat with her and two other stutterers in a tiny classroom. She taught us to sing what we wanted to say. It's impossible to stutter while singing. She never humiliated us. Soon, my psychologist noticed the improvement. It felt like somebody had pried a metal trap off my mouth.

My brother saw a woman shrink. And because our psychologists and the Toot were all in Philadelphia, we packed those activities into Saturdays.

But for the whole year before that, I'd taken art classes every Saturday with Mrs. Williams—looking forward to them all week long. I wasn't sure if I'd ever go back to those classes and pushed them out of my mind. After all, Mommy was in the hospital. If I went along with the adults' plans, she'd get better. It was already happening. During one of our visits, she showed us photographs of Phil and me that she carried in her pocket. She said they were her medicine, making her better every day. I imagined our pictures had miraculous power.

Somehow, Phil and I understood our parents needed to be happy *together*, in order for Mommy to be cured (of what, I was never sure). So, we left her and Dad alone during the visits. Phil went to the gym, which stunk of old sweat, like Campbell's tomato soup. I went to find Peggy, to learn her bouncy walk and to braid chewing-gum wrappers into bracelets. I gave my mother one.

After Phil's therapy and mine—and after spending the rest of the day with Mommy—Dad, Phil, and I got home around dinnertime. When Zili couldn't cook for us, my father took my brother and me to his favorite diner. He fed the jukebox dime after dime, playing sad love songs. Although Phil and I hated them, we understood how important they were to Dad, so we didn't complain. They were *his* medicine. And even though he'd never cry in front of us, his eyes were red. He'd bury his face in his hands, as if trying to wipe it away. I didn't know what to do to make him feel better, so I listened to the songs, pushing my food around. The overcooked meat and potatoes ranged in color from monkey brown to moth beige. I disguised them with ketchup. This food was nothing like the garlic, dill, and oregano flavors—the greens, reds, and yellows of Mommy's cooking. When I used to help her in the kitchen—peeling potatoes, cutting scallions, deveining shrimp—I told her things I wouldn't tell anyone else.

Those days were gone. I worried she'd never come home.

CHAPTER 3
MILTOWN

The Friday before Mommy returned, Dad drove Phil and me to the florist to buy her favorite flower— forsythia. She called it *for-Sofia*. I helped arrange the yellow swords in vases and hurried upstairs to finish a drawing of our house, in colors of butter and flame. I crayoned *Welcome Home to the Best Mother Ever* along the top.

As I waited in my bedroom, a black car rumbled into our driveway. I yanked back the curtains. She slid out of her seat. Dad, Phil, and I rushed out to greet her and carry her luggage. She looked as if she was in pain, as if her feet were made of glass.

The next day, Phil's friends came by. They scrunched their noses as if I smelled. Then they left with my brother. Even when Phil was home, he seemed unreachable in his room, a floor above everyone else's.

Dad had *his* ways of cutting himself off. He worked long hours at the office and then the municipal building. When he was home, he was either writing on legal pads or holding a newspaper up like a gray wall.

If I didn't look out for Mommy, no one would have. I was afraid of her going to the Toot again. I'd hear her crying with the voice of a little girl my age. Although it scared me, I knocked on her door to keep her company. She welcomed my visits. Once, she called me over to show me something. On the nightstand, she had stacked two dozen Miltown bottles at different heights, like an imaginary city.

"Dean, look—I'm going to Miltown."

"What's Miltown?"

"Sedatives—they make Mommy feel better."

I told her I made pretend worlds, too. But I didn't tell her I was a doll god, twisting toilet paper into dolls, the way I pictured God made humans. I kept seventy-five dolls with names on their backs (four whole generations!) in a box under my bed. Some died of cancer and heart attacks; one committed suicide; another was stabbed. But most died of old age—I gave those dolls wrinkles and gray hair.

I was also the undertaker.

When dolls died, I temporarily buried them in the sand below my swings, sticking twig markers, so I could dig them up. At night, muskrats patrolled the back lawn. I watched from the veranda. A month later, I went back to the markers and dug up the dolls to see what death looked like: lacy, eaten away. Then, in a bathrobe and construction-paper miter, I waved a censer. In made-up New Testament Greek words ending in "on" and "os" (*angelon, kyrios, dollios, deathion*), I chanted prayers over my dead dolls, burying them in the creek's clay banks— their final tomb.

This was my private world, as Mommy's was hers. Conversation was where our worlds met.

"Sweetheart, why didn't you bring me juice? You know how dry my mouth gets."

"Oh, I'll get some."

"You don't seem to get it."

"Get what?"

"Don't you care about Mommy?"

"Of course," I said, "G-grape juice—that's my favorite."

"Sweetheart, are you making fun of me?"

Fear spun through my head. "Let's talk about Miltown. What goes on there?"

"You're not listening to me, Dean. I won't have you ganging up on me like this."

Baffled and terrified, I stared at the floor.

"If your father was here, you wouldn't talk to me this way." She started sobbing again and asked if I wanted her to have another nervous breakdown. "Don't you understand how much I love you?" she asked. "Even in a crowded room, I can feel your presence and know where you are."

"But Mommy—" I interrupted myself, afraid of making things worse if I got angry. I had to help her get better. So far I wasn't doing a very good job.

"Do you know how *special* our bond is? But you," she stopped to dry her eyes, "don't care about Mommy at all."

"Of course, I do. I love you bigger than the Empire State Building."

"Fine, I see how you are. I can't believe I never saw it before."

"What can I do to make you happy?"

I remembered my father asking her the same question one day when we'd gone for a ride. My parents had had a vicious argument about something I never understood.

Standing in front of Miltown City, I was powerless again—afraid that *whatever* I did would bother her.

"If you have to ask, you really don't love me," she said.

I couldn't hold back my annoyance. "I wanted to picture your magical town, but you can take your dumb plastic bottles," I spat. I was going to knock them down. Instead, I stormed out and retreated to my bedroom, where my cat slept. Stroking his white fur, I heard Mommy crying. I slid the box from under my bed, lifted the mother doll up, and said, "I love you."

The next morning, over breakfast, she seemed chipper, as if she'd forgotten the incident. I hadn't. Asking to go back to my bedroom, I sulked.

Mommy knocked on my door and stuck her head in with a smile. Great news! That Saturday, she was driving me back to art classes with Mrs. Williams. I guessed this was my mother's apology. My head reeled with anticipation. The days couldn't go fast enough.

When we got to Rancocas Woods, New Jersey, I hugged my art teacher. She told me and two other students to climb into her car, its ashtray crammed with butts. My mother said she'd be back to drive me home. Mrs. Williams drove us to the countryside, where trees' colors seemed to have no edges, bleeding into sky. *Alizarin crimson, raw ocher*—I loved those words. We stopped at an abandoned farm. Stepping on pods dropped by "stinko" trees, the other kids and I giggled, accusing each other of having farted. Each ginkgo tree looked like the Greek letter Ψ.

Mrs. Williams told us to scout out what we wanted to paint. I pushed my easel into dirt in front of the white farmhouse. Drawing on the canvas, I squeezed oil paint onto my palette. Our art teacher complimented my ability to find secret colors—a rosy, ash-colored roof, which other students simply painted gray.

Back at Mrs. Williams's house, my mother waited in

her car. As she drove me home, I gushed about how my art teacher had praised my talent for finding hidden colors, and how she taught us to see the air between things—the blue between branches. Between mother and son, I did not say.

Chapter 4
The Ban

Home was 413 Wayne Drive. My mother said the four stood for our family, but the thirteen was unlucky. Our clapboard house was one among many on a curving street. In the summer, I'd hear the *ca-ching* of children's three-wheelers and the singsong of ice cream trucks. In the winter, carolers trudged through snow. A fire engine sounded its siren on Christmas Eve, Santa atop his throne, hurling candy canes to children.

Then that all changed. "The Ban" had begun. I was forbidden to step on people's lawns. Some neighbors hollered, "You can't come here!" or "Don't get any closer!" Some waved their hands, as if shooing away a rabid dog. The stretch of houses that had been my world was suddenly off-limits. I walked in the street.

One neighbor admitted Katie Hempfiger's mother had started The Ban. Katie was my best friend. Her mother was a Girl Scout leader and choir director. Somehow, this wholesome woman decided that because my mother spent time in a mental hospital, she had crazy-germs. Worse yet, I was a "carrier," a seven-and-a-half-year-old threat. The tall words of adults were law.

In summer, zoysia-grass lawns looked like claws. Maybe our neighbors knew that I thought about Jesus draped on the cross, finding him beautiful, wanting to hold him. Maybe I *was* evil and deserved to be treated like a rabid dog.

Katie didn't think so. We were still friends at school.

In November, we bounded out of the school bus near our houses. Giggling, I followed her onto her lawn without thinking. "Jeez, I'm not allowed here," I said. "I'll get you in trouble!"

"No, you're my friend. You stand wherever you want."

I couldn't remember when anyone had stood up for me like that. It's what I wished my parents had done when I told them a kid had punched me till I puked or that my teacher made me read, despite my stuttering. Either my parents were too caught up in their own misery, or they asked what I had done to cause these actions. That was the gist: I had brought it on myself. But Katie's reaction was different. I thanked her and darted into my house.

The next day—in the neutral environment of school—I asked if she talked to other neighbors about The Ban. She said she didn't trust them; they might tell her mom. She asked if I should tell the teachers. Some of them lived close by. Maybe they could do something. I said it would be a waste of time. None of them bothered to stop bloody fights that landed kids in the hospital. Nor did they stop bullies who tripped and punched me as I rushed up and down stairs between classes.

I made Katie swear not to tell my mother. If Mommy knew about The Ban, it would push her over the edge. I lived in fear of her going back to the Toot.

And even though Dad helped me with homework, I couldn't depend on him. I never knew if he'd be the father who could define any word I read or the man who buried himself in work. When he was *that* man, he pretended I didn't exist, working for hours on legal briefs. I joked, asking if they were lawyers' underwear. He didn't answer.

Hoping my silliness would get through to him, I asked who *Half O'David* was (my mishearing of *affidavit*). He still didn't answer.

He was stewing over an argument he'd had with my mother. At least two or three times a week, they screamed at each other till sunrise. Mommy cried in her canopy bed. He would sneak into the guest room. My room was in between. I knocked on their doors, asking if they were okay. They scribbled messages on folded papers, like origami birds. I passed them back and forth, but not before reading them:

"Ted, you've ignored my feelings."

"Sofia, I never meant to hurt you."

"I don't believe that."

"Sudsy, we're throwing away something precious."

After he used the nickname "Sudsy," her mood softened, but they still slept apart. Within a week, he'd whistle "Dearly Beloved," their signature melody. We were a family again, for a while. I'd wake in the middle of the night to make sure they weren't screaming. Eventually, that became a permanent reflex, disrupting my sleep. Nonetheless, my family was a world where I had some control.

People shooing me from their lawns was worse. They wouldn't even let me ask why. I stayed home, to watch over Mommy. The huge air conditioner breathed for our house like an iron lung. In its hum, I made drawings, dolls, poems—my radio playing. She had her Miltown pills, Plasticine sculptures, and Brazilian music. I'd lie next to her on the burgundy carpet, our arms outstretched, *bossa nova* music washing over us. With eyes closed, all hurt melted away.

There was another place where I felt welcome—Zili's house. It was the safest, most peaceful place I knew. No arguing, no crazy-germs. Eucalyptus leaves, arranged in Oaxacan pottery, filled her rooms with an almost-urine scent. She took me up to her studio and talked about paintings in progress as if they were people, "She's resisting me. Her hands don't know where to go. This one's a bad girl. I'll get her to be friendlier or else ..." A ghostly array of unfinished people perched on easels.

One day, admiring a painting, I almost heard music floating from it. It became a new way of seeing. I told Zili colors had sounds and vice versa, worried she'd find that weird. She said, "Of course they do. There's even the 'chromatic scale.' Notes have colors. And didn't you know abstract artists were trying to paint melodies?" To illustrate her point, she played an LP of electronic music, *Silver Apples of the Moon*. It was strange and metallic, as if it had fallen from outer space. Offering me a sheet of watercolor paper and gouache, she told me to let my brush dance with the notes. I painted a pewter swan skimming over ripples. Daub by daub, a perfect world.

A brush became a wand. The spell it cast changed Cinnaminson. By the time I was eleven and a half, The Ban ended. More important things had taken its place: marriages, graduations, a Swedish father's suicide. But what Zili gave me lasted. Unable to believe in anything as cruel as crazy-germs, she taught me art was as necessary as water.

CHAPTER 5
GUN WORLD

A pack of timber wolves surrounded a herd of caribou—teeth shredding flesh like red scissors. Watching *White Wilderness*, one of Disney's *True-Life Adventure* episodes, I pictured myself in Nunavut—an uninhabited part of Canada. Shocked by the slaughter, I looked at my brother. He was sixteen; I was twelve. Although an animal lover, he was engrossed in a magazine. Then, as if he'd heard something at a pitch audible only to him, he got up and left the magazine on the couch.

I ambled toward it and picked up *Gun World*. Turning pages, I read about parts of handguns: cylinder, trigger, silencer ... muzzle. I dropped the magazine as if it had bitten me.

Within weeks, my brother got hold of a real firearm, which he stashed in his room. How he'd gotten it, I never found out. I learned what I could from eavesdropping on my parents. Most of their arguments concerned The Gun.

Maybe it started with Phil's hunting trips with Dad and our beagle, activities I wasn't asked to join. If I were, I probably would've declined; as it was, I felt left out. It was clear, even if no one said it: I was Mommy's son; Phil was Dad's. And as the marriage came apart, the dividing line between Phil and me grew deeper.

He was a boy-boy. I was less than that. I had seen that look on my father's face the time I'd worn yellow pajama bottoms on my head, pretending to be Rapunzel. That paled in comparison to my lack of interest in sports. I found televised football and baseball torture. I preferred to watch a mime on Saturday-morning TV. Wearing skintight leotards, he taught kids how to paint and make crafts. The cringe in Dad's eyes said it all—I was hopeless.

At least he had one real son. They used rifles for their so-called hunting—shooting squirrels mostly, peppering their scrawny bodies with gunshot. Phil skinned and cleaned their meat, convinced it would make a delicious stew. I found the idea of eating them disgusting. Their little bodies remained in the freezer for months, alongside popsicles.

But the hunting rifle had become The Gun.

My father insisted Phil's fascination with firearms was a harmless boyhood phase. My mother countered it was dangerous and illegal. He asked if she thought *his* son was some kind of psycho who'd use The Gun on us. She answered that accidents happen too easily. "Ted, he's got to learn it's wrong!" she added.

"You're making a big, goddamn deal out of nothing."

"Nothing? It's a *handgun*, for Christ's sake. You've gotta take it to the police, even if he gets a record."

"*That's* not going to happen. Remember, I can make records disappear," reminding her he was the mayor.

In endless shouting matches, Mommy insisted Phil needed serious help, beyond that of the shrink he'd been seeing since her stay in the Toot five years earlier.

Because my shrink didn't think I needed to see him any more, I'd stopped going the previous year. My brother wasn't so lucky. He'd brag to me how he outsmarted the lady shrink. I secretly admired his brazenness. I'd spent

20

my childhood being a "good boy," and it hadn't gotten me very far.

Besides, his behavior was often sidesplittingly funny, even at my grandmother's expense. She visited us every couple of months, on weekends. Because she was a living connection to another country and time, I found her almost magical. Like Zili, she offered me an alternative to the world I knew.

She'd take me into the guestroom to tell me moralistic tales, with bleeding rose bushes and a cast of singing almonds, gossiping figs, and apologetic olives. Wilder than any fables I'd read, they'd been passed down from generation to generation. My brother called them "stupid old stories," but I was mesmerized.

Sundays came too quickly. We dropped my grandmother off in Mount Laurel, New Jersey, so she could take a bus hired by the Greek Orthodox Church back to New York City. Most of the passengers were elderly Greek women, dressed in black, the lot of them looking like a flock of caged blackbirds. As we waved good-bye to my grandmother, my brother balled up his fist, then sprang it open. Closed, open. Closed, open. His gesture was not lost on me—it was the visual equivalent of *Na pas ston diavolo* (go to the devil)! My parents didn't notice Phil's ongoing antics, but the old Greek women certainly did. Horrified at his blasphemy, they crossed themselves in unison, their arms a dark blur. By the time my parents noticed what he'd been doing, I was doubled over with laughter. Upset at first, they ended up finding it funny. Phil could always make me laugh. Maybe The Gun obsession was some kind of joke.

But then I wondered if Mommy knew something bad about him that I didn't see. Or didn't want to—the way my father refused to acknowledge anything was wrong. If she *was* right, would Phil suddenly kill us in the middle of the night? I pictured bullets blasting through our skulls, our white pillowcases splattered with spidery brain matter, the pillows heavy with blood. I convinced myself that wasn't the brother I knew. He had, after all, a need to nurture.

Take his pets. In addition to his menagerie of beagle, crow, cockatiel, and piranha (to which he fed live goldfish, nicked with a scalpel), he also kept pigeons in a coop. The scene in *On the Waterfront*, with Marlon Brando doting on his pigeons, reminded me of my brother. Showing me newborn squabs, Phil nourished sickly ones with an eyedropper.

Once, a white fantail escaped the coop and flew into our garage. Phil hadn't noticed. The bird perched on the door's track when Dad came home from work. Opening the garage door, he inadvertently forced the metal rollers over the bird's neck, decapitating it. Phil buried the pigeon, mourning for weeks.

I didn't believe a person like that was capable of killing us. But still, living beneath a loaded pistol terrified me. Sometimes, I'd wake in the middle of the night, shellacked with sweat, picturing its muzzle aimed at my head. I wanted a heavy-duty lock on my door, but Dad wouldn't allow it, saying I had nothing to be afraid of.

Phil's firearm wasn't the only thing that put me on edge. My parents' arguments could blow up at any moment; I never knew what started them. Mom would roar my father's name, "Ted, how *could* you?" He'd ignore her, giving her the silent treatment. The more he did so, the louder and more determined she became, burning through his frozen exterior until *his* anger exploded. One of them would punctuate their yelling by breaking into tears, shattering glasses, or cooing, "I love you." Within minutes, the screaming began again. One thing's for sure—the arguments contained the same two words, *The Gun.*

Unable to sleep, my brother and I dragged our pillows and blankets to the car in the driveway, wool trailing behind us on the ground, the seats of the Cadillac accommodating our temporary beds. My parents never noticed we'd left the house. I'd turn to Phil to share our predicament. But a dull look filled his eyes. In those moments, he talked in a gravelly monotone about the inner workings of miniature trains. I listened, knowing if I said nothing, he'd eventually stop. I didn't dare tell him our parents' argument wouldn't have happened if it weren't for his stupid Gun.

Eventually, instead of getting rid of it, Mommy told me Dad hid it in her underwear drawer. Then, she claimed, it disappeared. I'm not exactly sure when the crisis ended, but my father and brother won that battle, widening the divide between my mother and Phil. Emboldened, he wasted no time rubbing it in.

Two days later, upon entering our house, I heard her pounding on the basement door. Mom threatened Phil, saying he'd be sent to military school if he didn't let her out. He'd locked her in the basement and called her a bitch. He'd had enough of her crap—*he* was in charge. He laughed at her sobs.

Although scared of upsetting him, I yelled, "Mommy, are you okay?"

"Dean, is that you? Call the police!"

"I wouldn't try that if I were you, not if you want to see your next birthday, little Deanie," he said. I pictured he had The Gun on him, having never believed it was gone. At the very least, I knew he'd punch me; he'd done that before. My fear of him was greater than my concern for her. Besides, she was an adult. And it was almost five o'clock—my father would be home soon.

"Mom, I'm here, but I can't do anything. Dad'll be—"

"Dean, shut your trap!" my brother said.

But the pounding continued. Finally, she rammed a two-by-four through the flimsy wooden door. As her hand poked out to unlock the doorknob, Phil, wanting to be in control, unlocked it. She was eye-to-eye with him. "I hope you get how serious this is. When your father comes home—"

"He'll what? Tell me. I'm all ears," my brother said.

She ran upstairs to her bedroom, where she locked herself in by choice. When Dad came home, there was a lot of quiet, angry chewing over dinner, which he ordered in because my mother didn't feel like cooking. I couldn't finish my portion and asked to be excused to do homework. I was boiling mad because of the way she was treated. Mad because of the way I was ignored. My routinely being on the honor roll meant nothing compared to Phil's achievements: owning The Gun, locking up our mother. He did things I couldn't dream of doing, much less getting away with.

While I was in my bedroom, she was next door in

hers. Dad and Phil had "The Discussion" in the rec room. I wondered why she wasn't involved. But the Dad/Phil alliance ruled. Mom and I had grown used to our lower status.

Phil received his punishment: My father bought him a car, a green Austin Healey. He wasn't even eligible to drive for another six months.

Chapter 6
Mute

I knocked on Mom's door. She wanted to stay in bed and didn't feel like talking. I overheard her speaking—either to someone on the phone or herself. I asked if she was okay. "Yes, sweetheart," she said. But I knew she wasn't eating. So I made her toast, slathered in honey, sprinkled with cinnamon. Her eyes lit up, which made me happy.

While Phil never discussed imprisoning her and getting rewarded for it, he and my father tried to apologize by spiffing up the lawn. Despite what went on inside our house, we made the outside look pristine. It was the Mayor's House. Our parents had encouraged Phil and me to make our own gardens. In addition to weeding them, we clipped the Japanese maples, and took care of the yard. Phil rode on a lawnmower with a seat, like a throne. As he zoomed through grass, it sprayed the air with green arcs.

My task was to edge the curb. Cutting with a hoe, I switched to a tool that looked like a pizza cutter, and trimmed the grass with a shear. I clipped each blade, sweeping the excess into a cardboard box. Then I did it again. When there was no traffic, I'd cross the street to get an overall view. But I kept finding imperfections: too shaggy or asymmetrical.

Meanwhile, Phil had already finished mowing the lawn. He was indoors, the lawnmower parked in the garage. Eight o'clock: I sat clipping blade by blade, running across the street to see if it was finally perfect. I might impress Dad.

Nine o'clock: He came outside and said the edge looked better than it ever had and, that I should come inside to watch TV. It was dark; a car could hit me. But it was all worthwhile. He had complimented me.

Inside, they had opened the convertible couch. Propped on pillows, Mom, Dad, and Phil reclined under the sheets. I was happy to see her out of her bedroom and talking again. The sheet hung over the foot of the convertible. I created a private tent underneath it, separate but still a part of my family. As we watched a *Perry Mason* rerun—a show Dad loved—I thought things were improving. He and Phil seemed cheerful, even funny. Maybe I'd misjudged them. When the show ended, Dad said we had to get ready for bed. The following morning, we were driving to Philadelphia for marriage counseling.

Unable to sleep, I got up early and worked on my garden. Dad was putting out trash when he saw me. At first, he just watched. I broke the silence, saying I was happy Mom was feeling better. He said I was lucky to still have my mother. I asked him about his, realizing he'd never mentioned his own mother. He said she'd been a refugee from a place called Asia Minor. Their friends and family were slaughtered in a war. When his parents finally got to America, they lived in East Harlem. Unable to picture how they'd suffered, I asked what his childhood there was like. "Rough," he said. He was even stabbed in the back with an ice pick, protecting his sister from a rapist.

The punches and kicks I received at school seemed tame compared to that. I stopped snapping off brown leaves and looked at him as he spoke—seeing a part of him I'd never imagined. Instead of his sister's appreciating his heroism, she shouted out the window for neighbors to hear, "Teddy's a mama's boy." He explained that being a mama's boy could get a guy killed. Assuming that's what he thought of me, I asked why his sister called him that. He shrugged.

My attachment to Mom must've disappointed him. I had never even wanted to take "sides." There was no winning. Either I'd let him down or betray her.

But then he said something surprising. Like me, *he* had taken care of his mother—when she woke screaming from nightmares, when she pictured blood dripping down the walls, when she mumbled to herself throughout the day. Sometimes she described gruesome details of the killings. Later, she had a stroke. In the evening, he went to her bedroom. She unpinned her braided bun, letting it cascade to her waist. As she sang mournful songs, he brushed her coppery hair.

One day, coming home from school, he found her dead body, collapsed like a pile of laundry. The doctor never knew the cause. Dad said it became almost impossible for him to concentrate at school. He felt angry all the time. But he learned to tough his way through it. It made him strong; I needed to do that, too, he said.

I was stunned that he had shared that with me, as if someone I never knew had emerged from my father. The very thing that should have drawn us together—protecting our mothers—kept us apart.

Before I could say that, Mom appeared. Looking cheerful in white sunglasses, she said, "Good morning."

We waited for Phil. When we all arrived at the Philadelphia office, the marriage counselor greeted us. He said my brother and I could either wait in the playground or in the waiting room, where there were toys, books, and a kaleidoscope. Phil jumped at the chance to play outdoors. Even though I was almost thirteen, I stayed inside. I picked up the handmade kaleidoscope, unlike any I'd ever seen. It organized everything into glittering patterns. When the session ended, the counselor, seeing how taken I was with it, gave it to me. I thanked him as I looked at *his* face through the lens. Everyone laughed.

Trees and buildings along the highway spiraled through the eyepiece of my kaleidoscope—our car speeding home. A police car zoomed from behind us, its siren wailing. We never knew why.

The incident triggered something in Dad. Speaking in his lawyer voice, he shared an article he'd read in a law journal, "New York cops use a technique when a criminal resists arrest. The Adam's apple is so sensitive, if they shove it in, the guy can't move."

"You mean they jam it into his throat?" Phil asked.

"Exactly—makes him mute."

"Ted, stop it. This isn't the kind of conversation to have in front of the boys. Besides, it's making me sick." She turned the radio on to soft music. I wanted to speak up on her behalf, but Dad and I had made what seemed like a new friendship. I didn't want to ruin it. Even though I felt guilty, my need for his approval was stronger.

Phil continued, "So the guy can't talk?"

"Yep. But if the pressure's strong enough, he collapses."

Something snapped inside Mom. She started crying

uncontrollably with the high-pitched wails of a little girl. We pulled over to a gas station, where the only noncarbonated drink Dad could find was Yoo-hoo. Mommy gulped down her Miltown. Scared, we waited for the person we knew to come back. Dad cradled her. "It'll be all right, it'll be …" That gentle side of him was back. My eyes must have conveyed confusion.

"Should've kept my damn mouth shut," he mumbled to himself.

But she had asked him to stop. He heard but chose to ignore her. We all knew how easily she fell into that dark place where no one could reach her. *I* knew she was fragile, ever since the Toot. And I was only a kid.

I sat stone-still as customers at the gas station approached. Drawn to her wailing, they stared into our windows. They might simply have been concerned, but they made me feel ashamed, like we were freaks. Dad gunned the engine. The people scattered. My hands were red from squeezing them. I should've taken my Mom's side. It was clear: I couldn't be friends with both of them. Just when I thought Dad had a nice side, he disappointed me again. He couldn't be trusted.

CHAPTER 7
VOW

That September, I boarded the school bus to Cinnaminson High. We crossed "Bloody Route 130," a notoriously treacherous highway. It felt like a dividing line between a past I knew and a future I dreaded. I was entering seventh grade. The buildings we approached accommodated grades seven through twelve. Afraid of kids my age, I agonized over confrontations with older ones, who seemed more menacing.

I soon became the brunt of jokes I didn't understand, pranks (like cutting the back of my favorite shirt), and attacks in stairwells. I lied to teachers and my parents about an occasional black eye or bloody nose. No one probed further. I thought I'd brought it on myself but had no idea how to stop it. While I dreaded the bullies, I liked the teachers—except the dictator Phys-Ed coach. I was lousy at sports, with one exception, track. I was the fastest runner in school. When I ran, I felt like I was flying.

By the third week, boys engaged in Greco-Roman wrestling. The girls were off doing something else. As we waited on the bleachers to be paired with a partner, the boy behind me jammed his knee into my back. Hoping it was a mistake, I squirmed away. He pushed harder. I got the message: I was unwelcome. Someone always reminded me of that. Then I smelled something sweet, like blue candy. The coach finally called my name and my opponent's. He reeked of body odor, his hair greasy.

As we wrestled, other boys found it hysterical, making loud kissing sounds on the backs of their hands. Furious, the coach abruptly stopped me for getting chewing gum on the mat. He accused me of having dropped it from my mouth. I could never explain that the kid behind me had stuck it on my shirt. Identifying him would have resulted in my getting beaten by his entourage. I understood these unwritten laws. My default response: silence.

Nonetheless, watching boys twist and press into each other made me wonder what they looked like naked—especially the ones who taunted me. Shower time. I tried not to glimpse "down there." Boys made sure I overheard them say they were happy as hell not to wrestle with that "fag Kostos." Those comments started to sound normal. Survival hinged on absorbing humiliation.

It also demanded avoidance. I'd stay after school for band practice; I played the flute. Kids teased that I played the "skin flute." And while I didn't understand what that meant, I sensed it was one of the reasons for their attacks on me. When I didn't have band practice, I'd stay late to talk to a kindly teacher. I intentionally missed the bus. On occasions when I had to take it, students squealed my name—a busload in unison. I stiffened with rage.

When I got home, I watched *Dark Shadows*, accompanied by a MoonPie, and then buckled down to homework. New Math equaled misery. It made even less sense than regular math, but I was determined to get it right. I got straight A's in other subjects.

My perfectionism had intensified when my father, instead of being proud of my consistently being on the honor roll, said I could never compete with him. He belonged to Mensa. I had no desire to compete with him, with boys in Phys-Ed, or with anyone. I stayed in my room, alone, the radio playing. *That* was my best friend. I wished I could stay there all the time. I knew the songs played on my radio were the same ones cool kids listened to. So, I reasoned, I *was* fitting in, even if nobody knew it.

Over the howling guitars of "Light My Fire," I heard knocking on my bedroom door. Dad said I seemed upset and asked if I was okay. I wanted to tell him to leave me alone. But even though I'd convinced myself he wasn't to be trusted, I couldn't resist basking in his gentler moods. I didn't tell him about the incident at Phys-Ed. He'd be ashamed of me. I did, however, tell him I couldn't solve the New Math equations. I was my own taskmaster and wouldn't take a break until my homework was done perfectly—no snacks, no TV. Dad showed me a simpler way to do the equations.

He claimed to have been like me and suggested we go for a stroll, saying you can think more clearly when you get away from the source of frustration. We ambled down Wayne Drive, chatting till the angry knot inside me loosened. After we circled home, he said he'd bought a box of chocolate-covered strawberries and that eating one would complete the process. His caring moments managed to impart wisdom, for which I was grateful but confused, because that side of him usually hid from me. I wondered where it went or if something I did (or was) made him avoid me. I headed back to my bedroom, finished my homework, and went to sleep.

Two a.m. My parents' loud bickering woke me up. I watched from my bedroom window as Dad bolted into the dark, turned the car's ignition, swerved from our driveway. I assumed he was headed to the Oasis Motel—equidistant between our house and his Philadelphia office. He'd stayed at that appropriately named motel before.

Weeks went by before we heard from him. In the past, he'd stayed away for a day or two. It was already mid-October. Central heat gave off a hot-dust smell. Smudging grainy paper with the side of charcoal, I drew into the darkness with an eraser. Wraithlike figures materialized. Absence found its form.

Phil and I decided not to talk about Dad, not that we spoke to each other much anyway. My brother spent his time with friends, coming home late, reeking of cigarettes and whisky. Mom stayed in bed, crying. But I could no longer be her guardian. I was trying to hold back my anxieties that surged up from nowhere.

Eventually, she and Dad started talking on the phone. In a week, he slunk through the front door, briefcase in hand. He looked sweaty and defeated. Over dinner, we acted as if nothing had happened. I pushed my food, my stomach twisting.

"Don't you think it's time to repaint the dining room?" Mom asked. "I was thinking maybe olive green."

Dad did that face-rubbing thing, then walked to the turntable, and put on *The Mikado*. He drowned himself in Gilbert and Sullivan. Phil was seventeen; I was thirteen. Even though we usually laughed at "tit-willow," we chewed silently, understanding how much that music meant to Dad.

Asking to be excused, I fled to my bedroom to study

Mom's book of Aubrey Beardsley's drawings. One of my teachers had invited me to her wedding. Inspired by the book, I decided to give her a black-ink drawing. My subject: a dead rose, rescued from the trash. My mother found it morbid. But most beautiful songs were sad, I reasoned, so why not a sad-but-beautiful drawing? She winced.

My next project: a pen-and-ink drawing of a holly sprig. Mom said she'd have it printed and sent as our Christmas card—to friends, family, Dad's clients. I worked on it obsessively for weeks.

On the Friday before Christmas, she and Dad had driven to Philadelphia for a political party, their social life keeping tune to Dad's aspirations. Thrilled to be alone, I sat in a rocking chair with reheated chicken *oreganato* and a giant bottle of Coke. MoonPies for dessert. I was watching an old movie on TV: *White Christmas*.

Too soon, my parents' car pulled into our driveway. They stomped up the pavement, quarreling, something about her lavish spending. The front door flew open. They had never looked more beautiful—he in a tuxedo with slicked-back hair; she in a deep-blue, velvet evening gown with long, watery earrings.

"I told you I don't want to talk about it," he snapped.

"Ted, that's the way it is with you. Drop it when *you* feel like it."

"For cryin' out loud, Sofia, quit your yapping."

"Like a dog? No, if I were a dog you wouldn't ignore—"

"You have no goddamn idea what pressures—"

"Pressures? You?" With tear-blurred makeup, Mom unclasped her earrings, flung off her satin shoes, ran upstairs, her voice trailing, "You don't have much of a memory, do you?" She slammed the door.

I was furious at Dad for disturbing my comfortable world and for upsetting Mom. I was sick of forgiving him, only to learn he'd reverted to his cruel self again. As if I weren't there, he sat on the couch, Bing Crosby's voice warbling in the background. Dad loosened his white bowtie, removed his tux jacket, and grabbed *The Philadelphia Inquirer,* holding it up so I couldn't see his face.

Worried about Mom since her nervous breakdown six years earlier, I harbored distrust and hatred toward him. He crisped newspaper pages into verticals, releasing fold after fold. The turning of pages seemed to get louder. My mind started spinning. I tried breaking the tension, chatting about my day. He ignored me for forty minutes, finally sliding the newspaper down, asking, "Oh, were you talking to *me*?"

I became molten anger—for what he'd done to me, for what he was doing to Mom. I couldn't control myself. Words erupted from my mouth, "Why do you *hate* everyone?"

Kicking the wooden tray where my empty dish and glass sat, he snarled,

"I
don't
hate
anyone!"

The dish and glass collided midair, smashing onto the floor. I bolted to my room, never wanting to go back downstairs, never wanting to see him again.

A force took over. Heat thumped in my temples, pounding out the words: *Kill the hurt.* Neckties. I had a dozen: striped, paisley. Having learned knot-tying as a cub scout, I bound them together. I stood on top of a chair, looped the knot to a bracket, slipped the noose around my neck, the radio playing.

My thoughts blurred like sludge. I couldn't catch my breath—didn't want to. I felt like I'd split open my body. Everything sped up, the muck replaced by whirling lights. I was incandescent. Convinced that's what death felt like, I welcomed it. I stepped forward, lifting one foot off the chair. I hadn't paid attention to the radio, but at the moment I was about to raise my second foot, my favorite Beatles' song came on, "Eleanor Rigby." Its stabbing refrain, "All the lonely people," seemed sung to me. With the words of the song pouring into my ears, my mind thought beyond words. The music filled me the way watercolor drenches paper.

Then it hit me—one ally would be there when everything else abandoned me. Beauty: leaves shot through with veins. Beauty: a brush dripping with color. Beauty: light streaming from a painting. Beauty: a song keening from my radio.

I decided to live.

I didn't realize then how that vow would become a life-long credo. A warm sensation filled my body, a thread of tears spilling down my cheek. I loosened the noose, climbed from the chair, and stared into space. Everything blurred. An hour passed, maybe two. The radio lulled me to sleep.

CHAPTER 8
DR. SEX

A ll week long, I looked forward to Friday afternoons. School was out, followed by my favorite day. Saturdays, I felt safe, enjoying the expanse of free time. Because I finished homework during the week, I got to draw, watch TV, or hang out with Katie. But the night before, I'd almost taken my life. A residual numbness weighed me down. I felt thick and gray inside, like wet concrete.

The following day was worse. Sunday—the day before going back to school. Thinking about it made my stomach clench. Downstairs, a TV sportscaster growled details of a football game. If depression had a sound, that was it.

Katie called, saying we could listen to records she'd bought, while slurping down tablespoons of Karo syrup. She also promised to play new songs on the piano. She could hear a melody once on the radio and play it perfectly. As an added enticement, she said I could even see her mother's gallstones enshrined in a crystal vase. I asked about The Ban, scared her mother would enforce it, even though the block had stopped doing so. Somehow, her mother had forgotten all about it.

I told Katie I couldn't get out of bed. Maybe I was sick, I lied. Not wanting to worry her, I didn't tell her I felt like someone had yanked the bones out of my body.

I lied to my parents, too, saying I was doing homework. Instead, I stayed in my room all day, napping, listening to the radio, until, out of nowhere, a picture welled up in my head. I drew dancers with a black magic-marker on laminated paper. The drawing beaded up, and I laid Scotch tape over it. I then peeled the strips off, reapplying them to the window above my desk, like colorless stained glass. As day became night, car lights swerved down Wayne Drive, casting the black lines onto my walls like mysterious writing.

I liked being alone. Besides, there was no one I could talk to about having tried to hang myself. Dad scribbled on legal pads. Mom was too frail. I decided not to confess my suicide attempt to anyone. I was good at keeping secrets.

At least Mom had someone to talk to. I thought his name was Dr. Sex. It was Dr. Sachs, her shrink. While some kids' parents were religious zealots, my mother had become a devotee of a new religion, psychiatry. It could have been her reaction against her mother's religiosity, replacing a priest's authority with a shrink's.

Luckily, Dad's success as a lawyer made it possible for Mom to pursue her expensive religion. And just as she'd been forced to embrace to her mother's faith, we had to practice hers. Her shrink's unholy ghost floated around us, filling her sentences with expressions such as, "That's *your* problem, not mine."

But her shrink had plans for *my* life. The following week, my parents discussed what he had decided. Even though Dr. Sachs never met me, he reasoned that because I was the younger son, I'd benefit from boarding school. Far away, I wouldn't suffer through my parents' impending divorce or dangerous incidents with The Gun. He also doubted it had been disposed of. He was a man who studied human behavior and thought Dad was lying. Present or not, The Gun's sinister power lingered over our family in a phantom state.

I asked why Phil wasn't sent away. No answer. As for the divorce, we'd watched our parents' countless separations. I even told them how we'd slept in the car because their screaming kept us awake. Despite acting shocked, my parents didn't seem to care that I had to be shipped off because of their lousy marriage.

While they thought they were doing this for my benefit, I knew it wouldn't work out. I told them school was bad enough, but at least I could come home. I said if the kids at boarding school were as tough as the ones in my hometown, it would be a hundred times worse: I'd be trapped.

My parents had no idea how violent Cinnaminson High was. I explained how bloody fistfights broke out after three p.m. Kids raced toward the side exit, chanting, "Bash his teeth in!" If they knew the victim's name, they'd use it. What did it matter? The outcasts were interchangeable. I never attended the daily beatings, but a friend had. Hoping to protect the boy, who was beaten unconscious, my friend was too scared to help. The following week, the school buzzed with a horrible story: A boy had his elbow snapped back the wrong way by one of the bullies. I didn't believe that was even possible. I *did* know this: Every day an ambulance parked by the exit to speed maimed kids to the hospital. According to my friend, the drivers sat there watching, smoking cigarettes, making bets.

Horrified, Mom and Dad said they'd speak to the

school authorities. I begged them not to, explaining the kids responsible would retaliate against me. My parents asked if I'd ever been beaten up. I said I'd been taunted, punched, and kicked in the stairwells. It was the first time they seemed to show concern. I added I'd been threatened almost every morning on the school bus, which is why I walked home. Thanks to band practice, I left school late twice a week, avoiding violent older kids. I had become our school band's first flutist.

I pleaded with my parents not to send me to boarding school. They finally gave in, under the condition that I see an adolescent psychiatrist. The ultimate decision rested with him. I agreed to go.

Upset about the school beatings, my mother took me aside. When she was my age, she had fought back against her violent sister. Mom showed me how to use my fists. I doubted I'd have the nerve to defend myself. I thanked her and went to practice my flute. Trying to shove my anger towards the bullies out of my mind by playing "Etudes for Flute," I couldn't focus. Rage boiled up inside me. I got the embouchure wrong. I tried again: no sound. I wanted to scream. Finally, I snapped, "To hell with this shit," thwacking the instrument over the back of the couch until it bent. In that very moment, it was cathartic; but in the next, I realized what I had done. It would cost a lot of money to repair.

My parents added the incident to my growing résumé of troubled behavior. When the flute was finally fixed, I returned to band practice. Otherwise, I stayed in the library. I flattened my anger, quiet as paper, no longer raising my hand in class, except in Art or Advanced English, where I excelled. Those kids were outcasts, too.

I was almost fourteen. My nose was big, my skin oily. I felt ugly. But my classmates viewed me as something less pardonable: soft. Most of my friends were girls. Others were teachers. And even though they knew about the beatings, they couldn't get the administrators to listen. I usually stayed after class to talk to a sympathetic teacher.

But a January blizzard made that impossible. School closed early. On the bus ride home, kids chanted, "We're gonna wash Kostos's face with snow!"

I didn't know what made them hate me. I studied myself, trying to identify what despicable thing I said, did, or gave off, like a stench, so I could stop doing it. I could no longer simply *be*, like other kids.

As they tumbled out of the bus, the one who'd started the chanting—a short boy who lived up the hill—rushed at me, volleying punches into my stomach and face. The other kids circled us, cheering, "Get Kostos good!"

The snow's whiteness became a metaphor for my thoughts: I went blank. I'd had enough. I couldn't hold back my fury. Without realizing what I was doing, I started punching, kicking, everywhere at once. The short boy fell hard on his back. I jumped on top of him, pummeled his chest and face, his blood splattering the snow. The girl who had shouted, "Give that fag Kostos what he deserves," yelled at me, "Leave him alone. You're gonna hurt him!"

Then, the bully's mother called him home from the end of the block. Everyone laughed, which felt like a triumph. I released the bloody boy. As he got up, he promised to make my life hell from that moment on, vengeance when I least expected it. I agonized about retaliation the rest of the year, losing sleep. As usual, I didn't tell my parents or anyone else. I thought it was my own stupid fault. Besides, had I told them, this would surely have convinced them boarding school was the best solution.

While the boy never did attack me, every day on the bus, the same kids chanted my name in an effeminate whine: "Hiiii, Deeeeeaaaan." I lived under the threat of being beaten, as they delighted in reminding me. I'd get kneed in the back so hard I'd almost puke or have the strings on my hood yanked around my neck. On the rare occasion when my brother took the same bus, he came to my defense. The rest of the time, I put up with the kids' tyranny, waiting to go home.

There, I wrote angry letters, but never delivered them. I put an aluminum baking sheet in the middle of my bedroom, burning the letters, grumbling things I'd never dare say in person: *You're a stupid asshole! I can't wait till you die! Someday, you'll be afraid of me!* The letters dissolved into ash. Performing a ceremony made my anger less scary—even honorable. But Mom smelled the smoke. My "rituals" became the topic of conversation for weeks. Would I burn the house down? Was I the one to be afraid of? Secret discussions took place between my parents and Dr. Sachs.

As promised, Mom and Dad trundled me off to see the new shrink. He was convinced arson was not in me. In fact, he said there was something healthy in what I was doing: sublimating anger in a harmless fashion. He did suggest, however, that I do similar burnings in the fireplace or by the creek. But even though he sided with me, I couldn't get him to convince my parents not to send me to boarding school. To the contrary, he told them it was an excellent idea, wagging his head back and forth, emphasizing the severity of my predicament.

I never felt comfortable with confrontations, using words or fists. The one time I'd fought back resulted in constant fear; it crawled into my pores and became a part of me. Worse yet, I was terrified of my own anger—of expressing it to the people who made it seethe. So, I tried a different approach. I presented my case logically, as I imagined Dad argued in court. I reminded my parents my grades were excellent (except in Math), I didn't get in trouble, and teachers liked me (except in Phys-Ed). Still stunned by my description of Cinnaminson High's violence, my parents used that as justification for sending me to boarding school.

"But what if the kids there are as bad or worse?" I asked.

Mom and Dad said the administrators had assured them it was a peaceful, disciplined environment. I didn't believe it. Worse yet, my new shrink spouted some mumbo-jumbo about fourteen being an ideal time to separate from my family, given their problems. Despite my reasoning, my parents wouldn't budge—the shrink's words supporting their stubbornness.

Dad's turning on me was no surprise. But he and Mom had formed an alliance. I had worked so many years to get them back together, only to see them unite against me. Mom's blind allegiance to the shrinks was infuriating. All I asked was for her to protect me as I'd spent years protecting her. I had humiliated myself enough, trying to get them to see my point. From that point on, I wouldn't share my feelings or fears with either of them. I'd have to protect myself by myself.

CHAPTER 9
THE PLAN

Having researched schools for months, my parents finally picked one: Bakely Academy, a supposedly reputable boarding school in the rolling hills of upstate New York. Before I went, Mom bought me a green, plaid wool blanket, embroidering my name in red letters along the hem, so it wouldn't be lost or stolen. It wasn't, but by my second day at the boarding school, my other belongings started to disappear. I came back from lunch, where all the students were supposed to meet. The shyness I usually hid from everyone surfaced. I felt like my face was turned inside out and everyone was staring. The more awkward I became, the more kids elbowed each other and pointed. Avoiding their eyes, I excused myself. But they were on to me.

It began with little acts of cruelty: stealing a box of fudge Mom had sent me from Cinnaminson. I'd find missing book reports: one stuck together with chewing gum, another torn to shreds. Some primitive code had marked me as the valid brunt of harassment.

And even though our dorm had a sign reading *Males Only*, adults never supervised. Boys were there having sex with girls. Their whimpering sounded like Mom's cries. It took very little time for my classmates to realize I wasn't interested in sex with the opposite gender. I tried to act like the shadow I had been at my old school. But instead of having my own bedroom to retreat to, I searched for secluded areas in the dorm's attic. There, I kept to myself in the evening, until it was time for bed.

In the morning, I showered with other nude boys. Someone caught me looking. I knew that sealed my fate. From that point on, I bathed after breakfast—alone.

That night, my roommate and a group of kids barged into my room. They shone flashlights in my face, shouting, "Hey, Kostos, get the fuck outta bed!" Startled from sleep, I laughed, hoping they'd like me if I showed I was a good sport. I tried to act like someone else, or better—no one at all. Those skills had worked for me, after a fashion, at Cinnaminson High. Why weren't they working here? What was I doing wrong? That inside-out feeling wouldn't go away.

Yet I couldn't rely on my parents. They'd ditched me in this place. If I complained, they'd repeat more gibberish from the shrinks.

With merciless discipline, I'd build up my inner strength and self-confidence. Convinced I'd brought the harassment on myself, I was just as sure I could reverse it, getting the kids to like me. They were all I had. The following evening, after dinner, they gathered by the fireplace in our dorm. I'd show I was cool if I joined them. I pushed aside the nagging sense of being a fraud.

Addressing an audience of boys and girls, my roommate said, "I can blow cigarettes out my ass. That's why I got stains on my underwear. Right, Kostos?"

I said nothing, smiling as if I got his crude joke. But I was burning inside, wishing I could *will* myself to be liked or, better yet, disappear. I was terrified I'd stutter again. It could flare up if I was nervous.

"Answer the man, you been checkin' out his butt? Get it, butt?" a kid laughed.

"Listen, I'm having a rough time with an essay. You guys are funny, but I, I—" I stopped myself, feeling the rubbery clench on my lips that preceded a stutter. Kids giggled.

"Hey, Kostos, ever fucked a chick?" a boy asked. The girls in the group giggled, approving or uneasy. I wasn't sure. That boy had his hand inside his girlfriend's cardigan, squeezing her breast as nonchalantly as one might fidget with a set of keys.

"There's a fuckin' stink in this dorm," another kid said.

"Eau de fag!" a girl added.

"I smell it too," a boy hissed. "Fee, fie, foe, fum!" The group laughed.

The guy squeezing his girlfriend's breast said, "What ya think, Kostos? Smell it?"

I tried to act calm. "Think? They're fuckin' disgusting—fags, that is. If there are any around here, make sure you—"

"How do we know you ain't one of 'em? Never seen you with a chick. We got you pegged as a cocksucker. Hear you been checkin' guys out in the shower."

"Bullshit," I said. "I told ya, I *hate* fags. Fuckin' disgusting." And I believed it. I wouldn't acknowledge that's what I was, least of all to myself.

"So, what's your fuckin' excuse?"

"Leslie, my girlfriend. She's coming for Thanksgiving. We're committed and—"

"Aw ... so romantic," one of the girls cooed.

The guy with his hand in his girlfriend's cardigan said, "Time'll tell. If there ain't no Leslie, there's always the burlap bag."

"Bag?" I said.

"Yep, a whole lotta fun—for us at least. See, we tie you up in it and take turns kickin'. Great exercise!"

Another boy added, "The last kid suffocated. Oops! A harmless prank gone wrong. Nobody got in trouble."

I didn't want to find out if that was true. "C'mon guys, I gotta finish an essay on *To the Lighthouse*, and it's hard."

"Yeah, I bet it's *hard*," a kid said.

My roommate added, "Lucky me, sharin' a room with a perv."

I hoped he'd ask to be reassigned but didn't tell him. After all, he'd insisted I say *please* before speaking to him, or he'd break my nose. "Look, I gotta finish the essay," I said, walking up the slate stairs. As I headed to my room, two boys came from behind and pushed me down the steps. I hit my shoulder on a flagstone ledge and curled into myself, thinking, *Okay, I'm the loser you think I am. Leave me the fuck alone.* Footsteps and laughter. A scratchy fabric covered my head. Laughing harder, kids pulled another bag around my body, kicking me. I balled up, covering my face. The kicks to my back felt hot.

And this too shall pass. My grandmother's embroidered motto had hung in our dining room. I found shelter in those words. All events have boundaries beyond which they cease to exist. I dug my nails into my palm as hard as I could to make myself focus: *And this too shall pass.* But it didn't help. Choking on my own spit, I couldn't catch my breath. My wheezing grew louder until one of the girls made them let me out. She said she didn't want to get in trouble if I died.

The kids' attack unleashed memories of neighbors

claiming I had crazy-germs. Even though I convinced myself it made no sense, people's actions said otherwise. Being seen as some kind of mutant followed me to upstate New York. Maybe there *was* something horribly wrong with me, but I couldn't fix it.

I had *one* idea—suicide. That's the terrible thing about having tried it: The option forever dangles above you as a tantalizing solution.

That night, when I closed my eyelids, I saw dark teeth gnashing, taking me in. I couldn't sleep, worried the kids would break into my room. With nothing but ironclad will, I returned to my grandmother's phrase, breathing it in again and again, until I was dizzy—digging nails into my palm to focus. Bleeding, I fell asleep.

Next morning—six-thirty a.m.—breakfast duty at Mess Hall. Every student had a chore. It was supposed to build camaraderie. I stood next to my roommate. It was as if he represented every regular guy in the world. If I could be like him, I'd be cured of what I was becoming. Killing my body wasn't the answer. I had to kill this awkward, stuttering person everyone *thought* was Dean. I was hell-bent on getting kids to like me. And who can hate a person who saves them the trouble by hating himself? I saw a burlap bag of potatoes. I said, "Hey guys, they're gonna turn these into mashed potatoes anyway. Let's give 'em a head start by kicking them."

The boy said, "Don't fuckin' tempt me, Kostos."

I was silent. In the following weeks, I pretended I wasn't there—like the space inside the outline of a murder victim. I spent spare time in the Art Barn, drawing and throwing pottery. In those hours, fear vanished. Because the art teacher was impressed by my dedication, he gave me my own set of keys.

I kept thinking about recreating myself. When I watched Westerns and detective dramas, it occurred to me *those* were men. I wanted more than anything to be like them. I made lists of their characteristics and why people admired them. Then I listed real boys and men—classmates, teachers, rock stars. I collected pictures from magazines. When I was done, I'd let the old Dean die: suicide and rebirth at the same time.

The other place where I worked on my new self was the library. The kids who hated me avoided it, so it was hallowed ground. Dust-angels swirled in the skylight. I'd stare at those patterns for hours. Eventually, I had to go back to the dorm and the kids. But before the improved Dean was created, I worried they'd kill me. They'd figured out Leslie wasn't coming.

Meanwhile, I had a friend. We'd met in biology class. Although no one teased her, she was a loner of her own choosing. She saw the kids as "losers." She wasn't my only ally. I had my biology teacher; she respected him, too. He led us outside to examine the forest. "Notice how most of these trees turned color, except this group here. Why?" he asked. They weren't another species. Nobody agreed on the cause. But I couldn't participate. I shut down, obsessively worrying about confrontations. Maybe *I* was another species. Sensing my biology teacher was kind, I told him about the bullying. He spoke to the dean, but no witnesses came forward. That attempt increased the severity of the attacks. I should have kept my mouth shut. Living in constant fear shoved me into that bottomless quicksand: depression.

Still, I looked forward to biology class. Our teacher integrated science with philosophy and literature. He had us inspect the gardens we planted. Some of us, lovers of van Gogh, planted sunflowers. When we got back to the classroom with notes and clippings, the teacher read "Bring Me the Sunflower," by Eugenio Montale. A line lodged in my head, "Life evaporates as an essence." Our teacher asked if we knew about reincarnation, a Hindu concept. I said I didn't, imagining not being Dean, but a whole succession of *me*'s funneling like specks of light into the future. He then read from the *Bhagavad Gita,* telling us that Einstein had proved everything is energy, which can't die. I felt the same warmth wash over me after choosing not to hang myself. With the noose around my neck and one foot off the chair, I had decided beauty was enough to live for. Again, my faith was tested.

The next day, our biology teacher announced an overnight trip to Kent Falls, Connecticut. He'd escort us. Attendance was optional. My roommate stayed behind.

In the park, we trudged up paths, reached the overlook, and peered straight down—200 feet. Despite my acrophobia, beauty obliterated fear. Cascades rumbled down boulders in a step formation. Pools mirrored trees in a fanfare of yellow and red. Later, we settled in for the night in sleeping bags. I'd never seen so many stars—a smear of light. The waterfalls' sound rinsed away dread.

The getaway ended too soon. Back at Bakely, I couldn't find my essay on *To the Lighthouse.* I'd written it with a fountain pen, intending to type it later. Before leaving, I had tucked the pages in my top drawer. I emptied the desk. The paper was gone.

Just then, a group of kids barged into my room: "Hey, Kostos, that sure was a crappy report you wrote. Good thing it ended up in the right place."

"Crappy?" I figured it out. I ran to the bathroom and found a toilet with three turds floating in urine. Beneath them—my report: its blue ink quivering in yellow liquid.

"Shit, man, he's gonna stick his hand in there," another kid laughed.

Gawked at and taunted, I fished out the pages with the toilet scrubber, flushed the foul mess away, and blotted the pages with paper towels. I found the process nauseating, but the prospect of losing my report as I had written it was worse. Although I could have recreated it from memory, I wasn't sure all the turns of phrase would come through. I hoped they'd impress my teacher. That outweighed the humiliation.

My rage at what these kids had done, were doing, and the sadistic delight it gave them, was more than I could express. I had programmed myself to be invisible. I had no right to human reactions. I believed this policy would protect me, if I strictly adhered to it. But I hadn't been disciplined enough. These kids' actions were a living metaphor for what I felt about myself—and they knew it better than I. This incident was a turning point. Not only was I not liked, I would never be liked. Worse, I wasn't safe, as the following weeks proved: ostracized, punched, and threatened by overprivileged brats. I considered calling home, explaining my situation—far worse than in public school—but knew it was pointless. I'd already told my parents this would happen, but they didn't care. I was on my own. After a month and a half, I had to figure a way out of this misery called Bakely Academy. I longed to be somewhere peaceful and safe, where I could work on my art, have a room to myself, and never worry about being bullied. I thought it would be wonderful to have a caring adult to talk to. I realized I knew that place. I had *been* there, visiting my mother seven years before. My strategy: get myself admitted to the Toot. While it might not occur to most teens to get committed to a mental hospital as a strategy for escaping boarding school—it was survival. I remembered the facility from Mom's time there as a serene oasis with tree-shaded grounds. Patients got three meals a day, rooms to themselves, and beds with fresh sheets. The Toot would give me a quiet place to recreate myself. I would become my own parent. When I was ready, I'd ask and would be released.

I set my plan in motion by telling my biology teacher I had tried to hang myself in Cinnaminson and fantasized about doing it again—both true. His eyes grew large, his voice tight. He gave me the number of a Presbyterian minister, who was also a psychologist.

I told the man about having been punched, kicked, and almost suffocated, and my fear of being killed. I told him when I closed my eyes at night, a picture lunged behind my eyelids: black glass, gnashing like teeth. I'd open my eyes to make the picture go away. But when I closed them, it came back—more ferocious than before. I needed to be in a place where I could speak to an understanding therapist, like him. I revealed things I hadn't told anyone: that I was too afraid to sleep and was becoming an insomniac. That I wanted to stop my painful thoughts by shooting a bullet through my head.

While unburdening myself, I was aware these details could get me out of boarding school. That was the point. I figured it would then take two weeks, a month, tops, till some shrink at the Toot would agree I no longer needed treatment. Where would I go then? Back home with my parents. Even *they* would finally understand boarding school had been a horrible mistake. Maybe they'd even say they were sorry. I wanted to get back at them for having ignored my feelings. Worse than being trapped in a nightmare where no one hears you scream, I lived in a world where adults heard but chose to ignore me. I didn't trust the minister. It was safer to scheme. I kept my motive to myself.

After meeting with him a second time, he agreed the school was doing me harm. If I took my life, he'd be responsible. He said adolescent suicide had become a silent epidemic. I didn't care much about the stats. It might have been more helpful to have known the risk factors: previous suicide attempts (yes); family history of psychiatric problems (yes); a family divorce (an impending one, yes); social isolation (yes); exposure to violence in the home (verbal violence, yes); handguns in the home (yes).

He asked if I knew that "homosexual adolescents" were more likely to take their lives. Boys especially. I shrugged. That ugly "h" word made me sick. I wasn't about to share my sexual feelings with an adult. Least of all a minister. Had I told him that I fantasized about hugging Jesus, he probably would've pressed some button, releasing a silver chute, plunging me into the caverns of hell.

Looking up at him, I said, "So . . . will you help me?"

"I'll write letters to your parents and to the school administrators tomorrow."

"Th-thank you," I stammered.

The minister-psychologist composed a written statement that got me out of the boarding school and committed me to the Toot.

My plan was working.

CHAPTER 10
SECRET ABACUS

Placed on an adult ward for lack of room on the adolescent one, I couldn't have been happier. I'd done this by myself—an accomplishment, even if it made my parents sad. I couldn't let on that it was temporary. Besides, everyone—including Mom and Dad—would like me better when I got done transforming myself into the new Dean. The Toot would offer me solace, what I needed to put my thoughts in order like beads on an abacus. Surrounded by kind, elderly people, like Zili, I could change myself.

I had a task to complete. *Click-click.* The abacus-work would take time. I could reassemble my thoughts to resemble the men I'd designed in my head. I'd made a lot of mental notes—that man's sense of humor when teased and the way it doesn't bother him: *Learn from that.* That man's toughness—normal male behavior: *Learn from that.* Knowing how to be bold, to act like he belongs anywhere: *Learn from that.* I organized my thoughts, bead-by-bead: polished, logical ones; rough, irrational ones; scratchy, angry ones; scabbed, embarrassed ones; dirty, faggot ones.

I'd done enough work for the moment. Why not explore the ward? In the lounge, patients introduced themselves in a way that was comforting, calling me nicknames I'd heard in old movies: "Sonny" and "Dear Boy." These adults were more nurturing toward me than I ever could have expected. As we chatted, I tried to observe myself—to see if I'd already made some changes. *So far, so good*. Because I knew the hospital from Mom's stay, the ward's layout was familiar.

Later, I heard the lunch bell and shuffled toward the dining area. The chairs were ugly shades of gray-green, gray-blue, and dull pink—all in a sixties-modern "bucket" style. Telling me their names and asking mine, the patients at my table were visibly saddened to see such a young person hospitalized. They didn't understand: I'd sort out my thoughts each day, till I'd finally be released. I wasn't afraid to talk with them, as I would have been with kids.

So, I should have been happy, but when I least expected it, fear blurred my thoughts. With the scheme to get out of boarding school behind me, I had to face the fact: I was in the Toot. Despite the kindness of my fellow patients, I was no longer free: locked in, locked up. Having difficulty taking in this reality, I smiled but couldn't speak.

I pushed my food around on the plate, chewing a few tasteless bites. The plastic cutlery made it hard to eat. Metal cutlery was forbidden, since many of the patients, myself included, were considered dangers to ourselves. Two tines broke off my fork and floated through murky gravy. I laid a napkin over the canned peas and stringy meat.

One of the men slid his bowl of pistachio ice cream toward me. "Here, fella, I'm not gonna eat this. Don't need the calories," he said, patting his belly. Band-Aids covered the tips of his fingers. He screwed his eyes into mine as he spoke. "But you don't have to worry 'bout that. 'Sides, you gotta eat something."

I accepted, thanked him, and slurped the ice cream down, fighting off my nagging worries. While the Toot had seemed like the ideal solution, I had to accept the possibility that it also came with complications. I couldn't come and go freely; I needed to get a laminated pass from a nurse. And just about every minute of my day would be scheduled. If I was late for dinner, I'd get no food. Although the Toot wasn't perfect, it was infinitely better and safer than Bakely. Then another thing hit me, which I hadn't considered. Being a mental patient brought back memories of visiting Mom in the same place. Confused feelings flooded my head. The easiest way for me to respond to this jumble of emotions was to nod politely and leave the dining area for my room.

On my way, I caught a glimpse of Peggy, the Clown Lady I'd met seven years before. She'd been transferred to this floor. Seeing her completed the flashback of Mom's hospitalization with one difference: Here *I* was, reliving her stay. Overwhelmed, I clomped back to my room, midway down the hall. I comforted myself: I was in control, already making progress. My new life would be wonderful, and I had that to look forward to. My nervousness faded.

I'd already unpacked my suitcases and started putting my things out. *Hey, this isn't bad. A room all to myself— not like that crappy boarding school.* On the Formica end table, I plopped a miniature set of drawers. The upper one contained a photo of my white cat. The second one contained a cushion embroidered with part of a psalm: *For the Lord God is both sun and shield*, a gift from my grandmother. When I used to visit her, we prayed at her altar. She'd swab a cross on my forehead, the cotton dripping with holy oil. I pretended to hate it. Fact is—I looked forward to it, feeling lighter afterward, like red softened to a shade of peach. This memento of her brought me comfort. Even though I'd only seen her occasionally, she always made me feel safe.

Next, I lined up a set of miniature books: *The Nutshell Library*. My parents had given them to me before Mom's hospitalization. Last, I put out *The Catcher in the Rye*. I'd read it three times and intended on reading it again—Holden's voice throbbing from the other side of the page. I hoped I wouldn't end up like him.

Overwhelmed, I needed to nap. When I woke, my door was ajar. Someone must've looked in on me. It was already getting dark. "Fifteen minutes till dinner," a nurse's aide called out, reminding everyone not to be late. I slid on my jeans and sweatshirt, shuffling to the dining area. Even though this was my first evening, I knew where everything was. Each floor had the same arrangement of furniture and even the same pasty colors. They hadn't changed in seven years.

I made an effort to chat with middle-aged and elderly patients seated at my table. They spoke to me with tenderness—a quality I needed. Unlike my peers at boarding school, these people wanted to be my friends. Their parental concern would help create the healing environment I needed. They would be my allies. Sure, I'd have to put up with the restrictions on my freedoms. But I was protected, and I'd get used to the Toot's routines.

"Everybody, time for Club Meds," the head nurse sang, passing out pills in short, pleated paper cups. However, she explained that antidepressants can cause depression in teens, so I'd receive no meds. Nonetheless, she toddled over to say I'd be meeting with Dr. Archibald, a specialist in adolescent psychiatry, the head of that unit.

"You're lucky," she said, "He's one of our best."

"Aren't ya bald?" I asked, wanting to make her laugh.

"No, dear ... *Archibald.*"

The next day, a sympathetic, African-American aide, who chain-smoked menthol Newports, guided me through a gleaming, underground maze of corridors. She had birdlike legs and wore saggy stockings. Climbing stairs, we surfaced into the Old Building, trudged down a carpeted hallway, and reached Dr. Archibald's office. With a worried look, the woman said she'd see me later and disappeared.

Click-click: Add self-confidence. *Click-click:* Subtract the awkwardness that makes people hate you. I knocked on his door. Grinning on the other side stood a man in his sixties with a wide smile and perfect teeth. His silvery hair gleamed, as if polished strand by strand. He had an aquiline nose and wore a dark suit with cufflinks. *Why is he so dressed up?*

"Feel free to sit on the chair *or* the couch," he said.

"You mean I don't have to lie down like they do on TV?"

"Heavens, no," his last syllable as much a chuckle as a word.

I guessed his response was intended to make me comfortable, to win my trust. Avoiding eye contact, I scanned his office. A bronze statuette of a naked Ancient Greek youth stood on his bookshelf. "Boy, you've got a lot of books about mental stuff."

"That's one way of putting it."

Before he could answer, I found myself fascinated with work being done by gardeners outside. My thoughts seeped out the window. I wasn't aware of doing it; my eyes found any reason to be somewhere else.

"Dean, what's wrong?"

"Do they really need that many gardeners to plant bushes?"

"What's *really* going on?"

Scanning his books, I said, "They're sorta sad about the way things turned out."

"*They*?"

"My parents."

"Think so?"

"They sent me to this expensive boarding school." I was fascinated by the sprays of dirt, spewed by shovels. Meanwhile, inside the room, I was trying to observe *myself*, to guard against coming across the wrong way, but my head started spinning. I clenched the armrest of the leather chair.

"Try looking at me when we talk. I'm not so unattractive, am I?"

"Guess I … disappointed them." My voice dipped.

"So it's *your* fault?"

The gardeners kept digging deep holes like undertakers. I pictured my own coffin—smaller than an adult one—carried out and slid into the dark throat of the earth. I pictured Mom, in black, hiding behind a tree until she became it, the way Daphne had shuddered into a laurel bush. Even though I was angry at my mother's betrayal, I didn't want to hurt her. Pushing my guilt aside, I grumbled, "Didn't wanna go to boarding school."

"Eye contact," he repeated.

"You see, this is all temporary."

He chuckled, "Oh, *really*?"

"I came here ... to ... organize my thoughts." I left out the part about being bullied and afraid of getting killed. I didn't want him to see me as pathetic. The new Dean would never say things like that.

"And how does one go about doing that?" he asked.

"All I can say is ... when I'm done, I'll be back to normal and they'll let me out." *Oh shit—gave my plan away.*

"They?"

"Well, *you*."

"And would you go back to Bakely Academy?"

"Of course not."

"Back to your parents?"

"Ever see an abacus?"

"Why?"

"I'm organizing my thoughts like that."

"Are you agitated?"

"What?"

"Masturbation can have a calming effect."

I gulped, as though a wet piece of gauze had bunched up in my throat.

"At your age the juices are flowing. Let's see, you probably wake up with an erection—a pearly drop glistening on the head of your phallus like dew on a plum." He seemed pleased with his profane lyricism.

"You read all these books?" I asked, blushing and furious, looking at him for the first time. All this disgusting talk was intended to provoke a reaction. Easy to figure out. Would I show interest or disgust? Any response could have been used to label me. My suspicions of his cruelty were right.

But I was the one who ended up feeling dirty. Not that I didn't have a shaky foundation for relationships with men. I never got over Dad's saying I "sickened" him. That's what Dr. Archibald's sex talk did—it sickened me. Like this shrink, Dad was a man of scholarship and logic. Both men, it seemed, believed in cutting me down to "build character." And because everyone respected them, their observations carried weight. Even if I had talked back, how could I have been right?

"I've rendered you speechless," Dr. Archibald said.

"No."

"Nothing to be ashamed of. You can tell me about your sexual feelings."

My words wouldn't come out.

"It's perfectly natural," he said, sliding back the starched, white cuff of his shirt, revealing a watch and tendrils of hair.

Silence. I sickened myself.

"Well, I've made you uncomfortable enough for one day. Can you get back to the ward on your own?"

"Sure," I lied, not wanting him to ridicule me further. He would be one more problem to deal with at the Toot, but I knew I could outsmart him. When I got outside, I didn't see the aide. Nonetheless, I found my way to the main lobby. A staircase spiraled out of view. Patients told me rumors of an eccentric, old woman—a benefactor's daughter—who lived in a sprawling suite upstairs. I heard she had her own maids and servants. I hoped to spot her standing at the top of the stairs with her gray braids undone, singing. It was said she liked to sing.

I rushed down the marble corridor. Darkened by age, grim portraits of past benefactors glared from gold-leaf frames. Out! Any defiance felt exhilarating. I sprinted across the lawn. Past the drone of lawn mowers. Past the newly planted shrubs. I slid open the glass-and-aluminum door, padded into North Building, and snuck down the corridor.

I hope I made the right choice getting myself locked up in this place.

CHAPTER 11
FLIGHT

I thumbed the button, got into the elevator, walked back to the ward. An aide unlocked the door. No one noticed my return. A group of patients drooped over the modular couch, watching *Star Trek*. Peggy sat alone to the side, carefully unbraiding yellow strands of doll hair. She was my connection to the past, but I saw something I hadn't grasped as a child: her fragility. Seeing Peggy brought back memories of Mom's stay. The past and present collided. I approached Peggy and asked, "Do you remember me?" Unable to focus, she looked up but wouldn't answer. Then she made an annoyed gesture, waving me away. I worried about becoming like her.

But I had a plan: I'd go back to school in Cinnaminson, where I'd be popular for the first time. I had to be disciplined, referring to my guidebook, which I added to every day. I was reconstructing myself from pieces of other men's personalities. I was both Frankenstein *and* his creature, suturing the new Dean together with willpower.

Joining the other patients, I sat on the end of the Naugahyde couch pocked with cigarette burns. Aside from me, almost everyone chain-smoked. A sickly haze hung above the room. Without realizing it, I had sat next to the man who'd given me ice cream. He smiled and asked how I was feeling. I welcomed his friendliness. But instead of letting me respond, he chatted nonstop about his son—how smart and talented he was. Despite my attentiveness, the man's brown eyes tugged at me, as if to ask, *Are you listening?* I nodded, trying to be a friend. Because he talked about his son obsessively, I started to wonder if the boy was a hallucination. I never let on, not wanting to alienate the man. But after listening for over thirty minutes, I excused myself. I hadn't slept well, I complained, and needed to nap. Sleep had become my refuge.

He said, "See you at dinner." He looked up with a forced smile, more vulnerable than I had previously noticed. I had seen my mother smile like that when I was a boy.

As days passed, I came to see myself as the sad man's protector, as I had been Mom's. He and I sat in adjacent easy chairs. The fiberglass curtains behind us were opened onto the grounds. The man liked reading Sherlock Holmes novels for their "logical reasoning." In this peaceful atmosphere, I added page after page to my guidebook. I never showed it to the man, or anyone else, afraid they'd find it strange and confiscate it. Luckily, as long as I followed the Toot's schedule, I was left alone.

Almost every day, I had O.T., Occupational Therapy. I wasn't sure what occupation it was preparing me for, but I loved it. The sad man had O.T. at the same time. I made a glittery mask to decorate my door for Halloween. He said his son was also artistic. It's as if the man were becoming my surrogate father and I his surrogate son. I couldn't have imagined a better situation.

O.T. therapists had us make decorations for the holidays, to help us keep track of the seasons. For Thanksgiving, I came up with an Indian headdress from brown and orange construction paper, scissored to resemble feathers. I asked the sad man if Peggy might like it. I wanted to get back in her good graces. "You never can tell," he said. He confided that he thought the lobotomy performed on her was barbaric; he shook his head in disgust. It turned out she loved the headdress and even slept in it. Although it was crushed, she wore it, quite regally, to our Thanksgiving dinner, which had been laid out at the end of the ward. Card tables were covered with cloths and decorated with cornucopias. I was touched by the respect with which other patients treated Peggy. No one bullied her for her odd behavior and inscrutable speech. While suffering their own torments, these patients managed to tap in to some deep well of compassion.

The following morning, during breakfast, Peggy ran over to the window, "Snow snow God's dandruff falling jumbly from a tumble of white sky." Many of us got up to admire the snow clinging to trees and bushes. Later that day, I watched it from the windows in O.T. By then, everything had been blanketed—immaculate, quiet. The therapist had us make snowflakes to decorate the ward with for the next holiday, Christmas.

As it approached, patients and nurses made sure I got involved in caroling from ward to ward. They knew I'd still be there—no excursion rights yet. And though my parents promised to visit regularly, the idea that I'd be spending Christmas away from home hit me. Then, the more I thought about it, I realized it would be a relief. My parents' fighting always intensified that time of year. My own suicide attempt had followed one of their outbursts.

And Christmas day was usually ruined by cruel barbs my parents snapped at each other. After opening my presents, I'd retreat to my room. At the Toot, I wouldn't have to hear their arguments.

And yet later that day, Archibald told me my parents would visit on Christmas. He detected my lack of enthusiasm. I told him this holiday also contained Mom's birthday, Christmas Eve. The double celebration set our expectations high, unleashing my family's worst behavior. To my surprise, he offered a suggestion. He said I could pretend I wasn't feeling well if their difficult conduct surfaced. I was here to get better, after all. A mental hospital was called an asylum—a shelter, a refuge. He told me to remember that. Who was this man? All of a sudden he seemed kind, as if he were on my side, the way Dad's moods changed. Maybe I had to reassess my opinion of my shrink.

Strangely enough, when my parents visited, they were on their best behavior, as if someone instructed them. Dad even feigned interest in me. When I told him I was painting again, he said, "Very nice." I knew he didn't mean it, but it was an improvement. Mom had that same broken smile I'd seen on the sad man. I wished I could reach inside her head to hear what she was thinking. But she hid her feelings from me. My parents treated me the way family members act toward someone who's dying.

Finally, we opened gifts. Mine were drawings I'd done of a horse chestnut tree with birds sheltered in its branches. My parents handed me a large present. I unwrapped it: a magnificent book on Vincent van Gogh. A brooding self-portrait graced the cover in shades of burnt sienna. This book was a world of its own, offering escape from the uneasy, small talk my parents were making. They seemed timid and embarrassed. We tiptoed around any emotions, never mentioning them, as if to do so would let loose a fury that could destroy us. Instead, I turned page after page. The tome even included letters van Gogh had written to his brother Theo—the size and shape of the actual ones, glued onto the pages.

It was getting dark, which meant visiting time was ending. Saying goodbye was fraught with hurt and fear—theirs and mine. After my parents left, I experienced what I called a "white mood." As if rising up out of my body, everything became distant and blank. I couldn't remember details of what my parents and I said. I'd had those moods in the past, when my parents argued all night.

Worried my "white moods" indicated something was wrong with me, I told Archibald about them the following day. He said there was a clinical word—*dissociation*, "the splitting off of a group of mental processes." I didn't understand, but I was somehow comforted to know it had a fancy term. He said they sometimes referred to it as "levitation."

Later, sitting with the sad man as he read a Sherlock Holmes novel, I asked if he knew about "dissociation." He looked at me and said, "Someday you'll be glad you can't remember things." I wasn't sure what that meant, but sensed I shouldn't pry. Seeing that I was taken aback by his answer, he changed the subject. He had a favor to ask. Telling me he was Jewish, he wondered if I'd help decorate a Chanukah bush, as his son had called it. The man heard I had artistic talent and thought I'd do a good job. As he and I draped the silver tree with blue lights and papier mâché Stars of David, which his son had made, I asked why the boy never visited.

"Can't."

"He lives far away?"

I thought the man was mad, because he picked up an ornament and, as if startled, headed to the window. With his back to me, he said, "No."

"Oh, so he's—"

"He doesn't live … anywhere."

I pictured his son as homeless then realized—he was dead. "Sorry." I didn't look up, busily organizing ornaments.

He told me his son had started experimenting with drugs. The man felt guilty for not intervening. A changed person, his son became moody and uncommunicative. Finally, he jumped off a terrace while visiting friends in a New York skyscraper. Looking up at me, the man said I resembled his son, which is why he had talked to me on my first day.

I told the man about Phil—how police had brought him home drunk, bloody, and incoherent. Those incidents almost always happened around Christmas. I explained that despite being hated by kids at school, I got good grades. I started to believe my success had been achieved at my brother's expense. "I guess that doesn't make sense," I said. I finished spiraling lights around the tree, tucking bulbs in so the cords wouldn't show. The man watched me without speaking.

Then he picked at the fleshy corner of his thumb with

the nail of his index finger, until it bled. He said, "I often wake up in the middle of the night. See him falling, as if he'll never land."

I didn't tell him about my suicide attempt. He seemed too fragile. But he already knew, having asked the head nurse about me when I arrived. She confided that I'd tried to hang myself. I was annoyed that my privacy had been violated, but didn't show my irritation toward someone I needed as an ally.

"Listen, I don't know what's hurting you kids," he said.

"I'm okay now."

"Well, I'm here for you if you ever consider it again. It would kill your parents. You hear me? *Kill* them."

It's what I wanted to hear: *I'm here for you.* I knew in that moment getting myself locked up in the Toot had been the best decision. Convincing him I'd never done drugs or even smoked cigarettes, I said, "I'm doing this thing with my thoughts, organizing them."

He looked puzzled.

"Just watch. I'll convince the shrinks to let me out soon."

Looking with disbelief, he said, "Well, tell me if I can help." He was too anxious to continue and excused himself.

Surprising me, one of the nurses began playing the out-of-tune piano. She filled the hallway with the unlikely cheer of Christmas carols. She encouraged me and other patients to join her in singing "Silent Night." That brought back memories of being in the school choir. I had been a boy soprano, entrusted with the solo of "Silent Night" at our pageant. I used to love singing. But as we caroled throughout the ward, Peggy added her shrill voice to ours, seeming to sing an entirely different song.

Days before Christmas, the same nurse had us participate in a Pollyanna—everyone giving something we had made at O.T. Mine was for the sad man. I sculpted a small bird, wings outstretched, either taking off or landing. No one could tell. Maybe that's why it made him happy—the bird could control its fall. He said, "Listen, my young friend, get ready for dinner. I'll put this gift far from harm's way." He carried my sculpture back to his room.

I waited for him to join me for dinner, but he didn't. While I ate overcooked meatloaf with plastic cutlery, orderlies thwacked the door open. A woman, strapped to a gurney with brown leather belts, babbled.

"What'd they do to her?" I asked the woman across from me.

"E.C.T. Y'know—shock therapy."

"For punishment?"

"No, she gets so depressed she sits in her own pee."

I said, "Must feel like sticking your head in a socket." My distrust of authority reemerged. Maybe they'd use shock therapy on me if I didn't obey rules. I wondered if the Toot was going to be dangerous. Then, I'd be out of options.

Shuttling down the hall on wobbling wheels, the gurney disappeared into the patient's room. Attendants ran toward it, rubber soles squeaking on linoleum. They stayed in the room for hours.

I tapped on the glass booth of the nurse's station. It was the same nurse who'd told me I would not be given antidepressants. Almost stuttering, I got up the courage to ask if the woman who'd received shock therapy would be okay. With a broad smile, the nurse assured me she'd be fine. Then I asked if they'd ever use that contraption on me. It seemed like torture.

"Oh, of course not. You're not at all the kind of patient to require E.C.T.," she said, smiling, and trundled back to her booth.

Not trusting her, I was terrified the orderlies would electrocute me if I didn't do everything right. Imagining that heat zapping my temples, I pushed the fear out of my mind. But I wasn't the only one to be upset by the woman's "treatment." In collective sympathy, the patients stopped talking; their voices replaced by hail pinging on the windows' aluminum ledges.

I slogged back to my bedroom, peeled the covers, slid into bed. Couldn't sleep. I felt like a smudged drawing, as if someone had erased my outlines. I imagined what that woman must've felt. I knew empathy was good, but too much was dangerous. No, the terrible electricity hadn't made me disappear. I looked into the mirror to make sure. It reflected the window behind me. In the illuminated grounds, I spotted a leafless mulberry tree.

As a boy I spent time after school in the woods behind our house. In the spring, I'd climb a mulberry tree. High above the ground, I plucked warm berries, savored their gritty sweetness—my mouth and hands stained blue. One day, after being picked on by kids, I fled to that tree. Plopping a mulberry into my mouth, I noticed a leaf. Such a small thing had never seemed so important. A strange awareness came over me: *God must know every vein in every leaf in every forest in the world. God must also count every vein in my body, hair on my head, and those of billions of people. He also must know every fear I have and is always there to protect me.* Everything became peaceful. I never forgot that experience; it healed me then. Thinking back on it healed me again.

Outside my room, I heard caroling and pictured my new friends on the ward. The sensation of disappearing had stopped. I felt whole again. Brushing fear aside, I reminded myself I had O.T. classes the next day.

I had been going to the art room since I arrived at the Toot, but there'd been no room for me in an actual class. Finally, a space opened up. The sunny space, with art supplies, was one of the reasons I wanted to get committed to the Toot. I remembered the art room from Mom's stay. I wanted to paint myself back to happiness. As sun streamed through the windows, it felt like a holy place. The smells of clay, paint, and papers calmed me.

The O.T. therapist spoke to me ver-y slow-ly, as if she thought I was mentally incompetent. But after seeing my oil-pastel drawing, she said, "I had no idea—"

"It'd be nice if they had real paints here," I interrupted.

"By 'real' you mean?"

"Oil paints."

"I can't be expected to order supplies for one patient. You understand?"

"You like Miró?" I asked.

"What's your name?"

"Dean."

Organizing poster paint jars, she asked, "What's wrong with these, Dean?"

"Poster paints, popsicle sticks, and all that artsy-fartsy stuff. It's insulting." Afraid I'd hurt her feelings, I changed my tone, "Couldn't you say it was for the whole ward?"

"As long as you let other patients use them."

"Deal," I said.

As days passed, I was sure she'd forgotten my request. Two weeks later, she approached me.

"Have they gotten the paints?" I asked.

"Yep, plus pre-stretched canvases and different brushes." Bringing me this news genuinely gave her a sense of satisfaction.

"Wow—they got gouache *and* oil paint," I said. I'd told her I preferred the velvety texture and smell of oil over acrylic paint. In preparation, I drew on the canvas: birds about to take flight, feathers rustling into leaves, leaves into flames. I oozed paint onto my palette. For the birds in my painting, walls and time didn't matter. They soared over them.

Older people at O.T. stood behind me, making sounds of appreciation as I brushed colors into textures and forms. How fitting to live among these people. Like old movies and buildings, old people had endured. Surely, they had had problems as difficult as mine and got past them. My grandmother had. Her embroidered motto had been a reminder of that. I too would prevail. It was comforting to imagine *being* an older person, to live alone, to make my own choices. I'd no longer have to live in fear of my brother's gun or being sent back to boarding school. As if some answer awaited me in the distance, I looked out the window. Naked trees were covered in baroque snow. If I angled my head, the window became a mirror. I pictured seeing myself as an adult—wanting to shatter the glass barrier between times—to hear the voice of the man I'd someday be.

CHAPTER 12
LOGOS

Archibald's door was ajar, so I let myself in. I always got to his office about fifteen minutes late, which we discussed for another fifteen. That was how I whittled away time he might otherwise have spent saying things to embarrass me. *I* was redirecting the conversation, and he never caught on.

As I sank into the leather couch, he swiveled his chair to face me and opened his legs. For some reason, he pushed his synthetic socks down to his ankles, making a prickly sound. Then he tugged his black slacks up. His legs were shiny. He checked to make sure I was looking. I couldn't figure out if he wanted me to be attracted to him or if it was a test, to catch me and say, *Aha! Now we know what you are.* It was impossible not to look. But my dedication to changing my personality made me careful not to give myself away. I had to annihilate the old me. I wouldn't give in to his probing eyes, his questions.

Was he just another kind of bully? No, I convinced myself he was offering me the perfect challenge. Stone-faced, I paid no attention to his badgering about my personal anatomy, my ejaculations, and my sexual interests. The better I'd become at ignoring him, the tougher I was becoming.

But my battles with him weren't limited to our sessions. I had a nightmare: It took place at the Poe House I'd visited as a schoolboy. Instead of one of the author's characters, Archibald opened the door, flames curling from his mouth. "I'm a sexy devil," he hissed. I slammed the door in his face, but didn't dare tell him about the nightmare the following day. He'd have gone on about *that*. What's more, it would've given him too much power. I'd figured him out. Problem was, he'd figured me out, too. Beneath all the sexual innuendoes, he must have perceived what I could never admit to anyone: My sexual fantasies were about older boys and men. I could never tell him how I'd ogled body builders in posing straps at the back of comic books. Worse yet, I obsessed over a sensuous, sad-eyed Jesus, writhing on the cross. I wanted to take him down from that horrible contraption and hold him in my arms.

My mother had a book of Michelangelo's sculptures. *The Milan Pietà* caught my attention. Christ's torso and pectorals excited me. The more I scolded myself—*I'll never, never think about that again*—the stronger the yearning became. I never told Archibald how ashamed I was of those attractions. I simply listened to his yammering, trying not to look at him. Somehow his need to show off his calves made me think back on an incident with Dad.

Going to the beach with my family, I had secretly watched hairy-chested men in Speedos, noticing my father eyeing them, too. He blurted out to my mother that he knew what kind of men they were and why they dressed in those "ridiculous bikinis"—to attract others of their "ilk." Unfazed, Mom asked him why it mattered. He said they sickened him. I'd heard that word before. But I didn't believe Dad found those men disgusting, because he looked at them the way I did.

I sat across from a man who reminded me of my father. Both men confused and infuriated me. And both were condescending. Archibald said he understood I was doing some "attractive" artwork at O.T. I questioned what he meant. As if it were an improvement, he replaced "attractive" with "therapeutic." I shrugged. He relented somewhat, saying the therapists reported that I might have some talent. (The word "some" stabbed my ear.) I told him I'd painted since I was little. He jotted furiously on his pad. I said my mother had a drawing I'd done of my room before I could speak—a sort of overhead floor plan, as if I were looking down from the ceiling. He said children are fascinated by geometric shapes.

"Maybe I left my body," I said.

"You were probably copying letter forms."

"Maybe." Mom had tried teaching me Greek before English, but that was a year later. My eyes skimmed over rows of leather-bound books, with gold Roman numerals. I wondered if Archibald actually read them or simply had them to look impressive, like his wall of diplomas. *How many fucking schools had he graduated from?*

He informed me he'd studied Ancient Greek.

"*Logos* means both word and logic," I said, "as if words organize—"

"Thoughts? Isn't that what we're doing?" he asked.

"But I also think in pictures." I said maybe it had been my mother's influence, and also Zili's, our neighbor. I recounted how I'd met her with my best friend Katie, on one of our expeditions. We'd marched to a house up the block, because the older couple seemed exotic, and buzzed their bell. A woman opened the door, a pencil securing her ashy-brown bun. Her eyes glinted aluminum. She told us her name and welcomed us in. I had never seen so much art. In her studio, we had to be careful not to step on drawings spread across the floor. Those images reappeared on nearby canvases.

Setting two places at a table, this artist gave us clumps of clay, telling us to let our imaginations go wild. As I squeezed the clump, a curve rose from an oval, as if forming itself: It became a mother swan. I sculpted two baby swans riding on her back.

Days later, Zili showed us our dried sculptures and the colors we could use to paint them. I presented my figurine to Mom for Mother's Day. She put it on the mantle. Archibald asked if needing her approval sparked my interest in art. Irritated, I said his question made my love of art seem fake. I reminded him that after meeting Zili, I wanted to go to art classes.

It started with Mom taking me to a movie house that played foreign films. I loved their mysterious quality. "At the movie house, I noticed a flyer: SATURDAY ART CLASSES FOR CHILDREN." Mom called the next day and drove me to the teacher's house every Saturday. Her name was Mrs. Williams. A plate of warm Toll House cookies awaited us. With three other students, I drew, painted, sculpted, and gouged pictures into linoleum blocks. She also took us to the Philadelphia Museum of Art. We entered rooms of other countries. One was a Japanese village: Iron-dark Buddhas peered from altars. We then walked along a corridor to the top of vast marble stairs. But looking down made me dizzy and terrified, my palms sweating. Fighting the temptation to jump, I darted into a gallery, finding art I recognized from Mom's books.

It was as if seeing those paintings "happened" to me. They were as memorable as going to a friend's birthday party or getting a guinea pig. Everything else had to be endured.

Archibald said, "That sounds like escapism."

"No, art made life *more* real." I told him how it manifested everywhere. For Christmas, Mom scooped out a swan from Styrofoam, studded it with lights, and covered the form with angel's hair. In the dark, the swan came alive with fiery spirals.

"Does she still sculpt?"

"Sure, with clay and junk sculpture."

"What?"

"We find broken things. An old radiator might become the ribs of an animal."

"Certainly takes imagination, something your father must not—"

"Well, I like words, too, even if he thinks my poems don't make sense." Then I realized, as if seeing it on a thought-page:

Father = Word.

Mother = Image.

I was trying to bring my parents together in Poem.

As if not hearing me, Archibald changed the subject, "Dean, it slipped my mind—great news."

"Really?"

"A room's finally available on the adolescent ward."

My jaw clenched, barely letting words escape, "The *where*?"

He said I'd be with people my own age, which he considered therapeutic.

I countered that I was happy living with older people. I even knew Peggy from before. "Please, don't make me," I begged the way I had with my parents not to send me to Bakely Academy. It was just as effective.

He answered by saying I'd already been on the adult ward seven months too long.

I added I was improving daily—no longer thinking about suicide.

"Then you'll get even better in the appropriate environment."

"But I *love* these people here."

He assured me I'd be happier with people my age. Legally, the Toot was required to make sure I continued my schooling. On the adolescent ward, there was an accredited teacher, Matthew. I'd go to classes every day.

"But I've been seeing a tutor."

No, I needed to interact with other teens. Blah, blah, blah. The socializing process. Blah, blah, blah. I was surprised he didn't say *therapeutic* again. I couldn't look at him, couldn't talk. He said when I got released I wouldn't have to miss a grade and would be more comfortable with my peers.

My plan was disrupted. I said, "So that's it? Even if I beg a hundred times?"

He told me to stop being silly. It wasn't going to be bad. Besides, it would also help with my *sexual* development. I didn't dare ask what he meant, but in no time he leaped to his favorite topic: masturbation.

Not getting the connection between the adolescent

ward and my sexual development, I looked up, without saying a word. He had a smirk, as if he'd said something clever. But I shut down. That was how I got him to be quiet. Worse than humiliating me, he was derailing my plan that had been working perfectly. I was fuming, the way I'd been angry at Dad and Mom. But because I didn't deserve human emotions, I couldn't show my anger, afraid Archibald might've made things worse. *How would he understand the importance of my staying on the adult unit, never having been on my side?*

CHAPTER 13
UNIT I

Boxes full of my paintings, sculptures, and pottery lined up by the door. After lunch, an aide accompanied me from Unit III to Unit I—from a ward for older adults to one exclusively for adolescents. Leaving safety behind, I couldn't stop worrying about the dangers I might face. Images of Cinnaminson High and Bakely Academy filled my thoughts. But I had no choice. The only power I wielded existed in my head. I tried to shove fear of the unexpected out of my mind.

Besides, maybe it was for the best. Time to spread my wings like my clay sculpture. I'd done a lot of good work on the adult ward—thanks to my caring friends. Their support had allowed me to focus on the transformations I needed to make. I was pissed off at Archibald, not that I'd give him the satisfaction of showing it. He'd be surprised to find out I was ready to live among my peers, the people I dreaded most. It was time to test my efforts. I told myself the changes I'd implemented would make people see a new Dean. I would *not* be treated the way I had been at Bakely. Those kids were right to bully *that* Dean. He was dead; I'd finished him off.

Now, the kids on Unit I would see me as one of them.

Before the transfer, the sad man scheduled a good-bye party for me on the grounds. An aide and some orderlies came, along with Peggy and an elderly patient who never spoke. I didn't know if she was mute, but she always drew me into her silence. She'd come up from behind, laying her hand on my shoulder. The first time I'd been startled, twisting around to see her gray eyes reassuring me. I never spoke to her, respecting her form of communication. She eventually taught me her "language." Other patients I'd never even spoken to showed up. I felt like Alice at the Mad Hatter's party. Peggy had braided gum wrappers into a chain, encircling our space, giving our celebration a magical air. That chain separated us from people who walked with nurses, sat alone, or argued with invisible enemies.

Peggy came toward me. Holding out a paper bag, she said, "I traded bracelets for diamond-stars and erasers don't leave dirty smudges nice boy the night an idiot savant I wrap you in the bag and keep you safe."

"Can I open it, Peggy?" I asked. She smiled, drool spilling from her mouth. The bag contained an orange, a pinecone, seed-wings, and a piece of paper reading: *TAY CARE.* I tucked her gifts back in the bag. "You realize, Peggy, I'll be downstairs on Unit I. We can still be friends." She started humming. I continued, "Let's consider this our special meeting place. Okay?" She kept humming.

Confused by the French-sounding phrase, *idiot savant*, I asked the sad man what it meant. He said it's a person who comprehends a lot about only one subject. He then told me one of the aides had informed him that Peggy had a Ph.D. and used to teach anthropology at one of Pennsylvania's universities. The story was hazy—something about her committing a horrible crime, for which she was lobotomized. The court ordered it. The aide either didn't know or didn't want to divulge details.

But from the word "horrible," I pictured Peggy hacking up her children. I wouldn't let myself imagine her doing something so grotesque. But it confirmed what I already suspected—the Toot was a labyrinth of untold stories and secrets.

"On a more cheerful note," he said, "can I give you my present now?" He had wrapped his oddly shaped gift in a Chinese newspaper with red ribbon. I unwrapped it, finding a bird's nest with a few tweed-brown feathers. I knew what it meant—his response to mine. My gift was about potential. His was possibly a reminder to stay close to people who'd look after me. Like his son, I could fall. I'd prove him wrong.

The aide said, "Dean, I doubt you'll ever forget your friends from Unit III."

"How could I? They've helped me get better." I noticed the sad man suddenly looked distracted, staring at the wall, chewing on the cuticles on his thumb. "We'll still be friends, right?" I asked him. I needed to know I could rely on him if something went wrong. I counted on the fact that he cared about me a little more than anyone else, that helping me was like holding onto his son.

"Right, right," he said, turning away, distracted by something no one heard.

Taking a drag from her menthol cigarette, the aide looked at her watch and said, "Dean, it's time for the move." Everyone took turns hugging me. When I got to the sad man, he snorted back tears. I wished he had been my father. Before I could speak to him more, I was whisked down an elevator by the aide.

Unit I was on the ground floor of the North Building.

The aide escorted me to the front door, which a nurse unlocked. When I turned around, the aide had vanished. Another one met me. She told me her name was Cora, short for Corazón. She was from the Philippines.

The layout of this ward was identical to Unit III: immediately to the right, the glass-enclosed nurse's station; to the left, a small conference room. Farther inside, the dining room with the same ugly chairs. Directly across from that, the same modular couches and a large TV perched on a pedestal like a fetish on an altar. *Bewitched* was playing, but no one was watching. Cora told me there would be a Morning Meeting: roll call and a discussion of problems from the previous day. Same as in Unit III. These similarities made me feel less uprooted, less afraid.

But despite the identical layout, loud rock music blared from patients' rooms. Most of the kids wore jeans. Some milled about barefoot, some with unkempt hair. As Cora escorted me to my room, I peered into others. Bright posters adorned the walls. My room was white: white walls, white sheets, white blanket. The starkness almost made my teeth hurt. But it had been the same in the other ward at first. And I added my artwork to personalize it. I'd do the same here. Iron grills, more like prison bars, covered the windows. I reminded myself we were on the ground floor. They were for my own safety. I convinced myself: *Everything is fine.* Sitting on the bleached bed, I mouthed, "Thank you" to Cora as she walked away.

Overwhelmed by feelings I couldn't make sense of, I became sleepy. As an insomniac, I'd learned to grab sleep whenever I could. When that velvety feeling of drowsiness came over me, I welcomed it. It also was a means of escape.

After waking from my nap, I explored the grounds. Maybe I'd run into some of my old friends from Unit III. No such luck. Instead, I watched the fat guard at the entrance to the wall. It hit me that the exit and entrance were the same thing, depending on your situation. For me, it was off limits. The stone wall surrounding the Toot was fact. In spite of my bravado, I had to admit my perfect plan wasn't going the way I'd mapped it out. I was only supposed to be here a couple of weeks. Months had lapsed, and Archibald said nothing about release.

The passing of time was marked by my hair. Having grown over my ears, it was level with my jaw line. I looked in my bathroom mirror. My hair—straight when short—was wavy, as if belonging to a different person. I dragged my brush through it, reminding myself the old Dean was a ghost. I needed to release him from memory. I had no room for the dead.

Time to put my transformation to the test—interacting with other kids. I wandered into the halls and spotted a broad-shouldered boy, about sixteen years old. He had lion-colored hair. The way he sat with a bony girl made it clear they were "together." This was not promising. It brought back memories of Bakely: students having sex behind adults' backs. That was how those kids had figured me out, seeing that I wasn't doing "it." In my attempt to escape that hellhole, I'd landed in another pit, thanks to my stupid shrink. Maybe it was my own fault, too—that is, my former self's. Nobody knew it, but I was his replacement.

Or so I hoped. I worried about stuttering when kids talked to me. If I did, they'd laugh, and I'd be stuck in another trap with no way out. I'd played my only escape card getting into the Toot. What would I do if *this* place was just as bad? Dread hooked into my guts. When I was afraid, it pulled taut. Otherwise, it slackened, but it never went away. I always felt its weight.

Alleviating my fears, Cora approached and said, "Dino, you've got O.T. today. I can't wait to see what you paint." I liked the lilt of her accent. "The O.T. therapists told me a lot about your artwork," she said.

"Really?"

"Yes. Then you'll have lunch and class with Matthew. C'mon, cheer up."

Her calling me *Dino,* as Mom did, made me feel better. The information didn't make me happy as much her concern. She even tried to get me to laugh. My only response was to blurt, "No," "Great," "Thanks," or any monosyllabic word I could force out. Speaking was too much effort. Besides, I had a stomachache, which came and went, as my insomnia did. Lunch sounded disgusting. But I was polite to Cora, for she seemed to care. I knew she could be an ally, as the adults in Unit III had been. I didn't want to alienate her.

She walked me to O.T. Because it was my first time with her, she stayed throughout the session. I enjoyed her company, even though I couldn't bring myself to chat. Depending on their states of despair or delusion, some patients were accompanied by aides or nurses. If the person was on suicide watch or had fallen into a stupor, the professional was there to make sure the patient wasn't self-destructive or idle. I wasn't sure if there were rules governing these activities, but I assumed they came from the shrinks.

I watched a woman weaving: Threads shuttled through corridors of other threads, spools shifting, changing colors until a pattern emerged. The passage was made physical in the cloth, like thought made physical by writing. She could choose the colors and patterns. That's what I was doing with myself, becoming my own creation. I even practiced making my voice deeper, more masculine.

I wandered back to the splattered part of the room where people painted. Finding the canvases I'd asked for, I gathered tubes of oil paint but couldn't decide on a topic.

"Why not a self-portrait? You have nice eyes," Cora said.

"But I need a mirror."

The occupational therapist opened a drawer, handing me a mirror on a swiveling base. I had to sign it out. It wasn't something they'd let patients take to their rooms. Smashed, it could be used for cutting. The idea of cutting myself, once explained, was more tantalizing than I wanted to acknowledge. I edged it out of my mind, staring instead into the "me" reflected: a peach-fuzz moustache framed my mouth. Trying to see myself as a new person—stripped of the disgusting qualities that had rightly caused people to loathe me—would my new self-portrait be an "I" or a "he"? I had grown used to monitoring my actions and statements. Gazing into the mirror, I fell into the black chutes of my pupils. Having no energy to paint, I stared.

Cora's voice, more like singing, pulled me out of my thoughts. She escorted me back to the ward. As we walked in the door, we were met by a trail of blood, a chaos of nurses and aides. Cora told me to wait outside with her. We heard the slosh of orderlies mopping the mess with disinfectants. Stepping over wet linoleum, I rushed inside, back to my room. I felt like the patient's trail of blood had seeped into me, even though I hadn't said a word to her. She was the girlfriend of the lion-haired boy. I sank into that familiar, lightless place: depression. *This is what worthless people like you deserve.* It took too much effort to pry myself out of that mood.

Finally, I forced myself past my sluggishness and opened the door, needing to be around other people. A hush spread throughout the unit. Cheerful TV voices and canned laughter filled the Day Room, where I wandered in hopes of making a friend. But everyone was silent. Those artificial voices seemed to mock us as if they were emissaries from a happy place, one we could never imagine. Without talking, we retreated to our respective rooms, where we stayed till the following day.

At Morning Meeting, I learned that Terri, the anorexic girl, had slashed her wrists and severed an artery. Her therapist wanted us to understand Terri's struggles so we could be more sensitive to her needs. We learned why she limped, her sharp-boned hips almost jutting out in jeans: She had leapt from a fourth-floor window years earlier. Pregnant, she had seen no way out. The fetus died; she survived. But instead of this information inspiring compassion for Terri, a few patients later taunted her, chasing her with wire hangers, saying they were ready to perform another abortion. I was amazed *I* wasn't the recipient of their bullying. It certainly made me feel sorry for her. I wished I could've taken her side, getting the kids to stop. I wasn't that brave. Besides, they could've turned on me. But they were afraid to bother her if her boyfriend was around. Then it occurred to me to become friends with him. His nickname was Lion Boy. He came to like me and appreciated my willingness to befriend Terri. My ability to create a friendship with someone so cool—the kind of guy who would've hated me at Bakely—was an accomplishment. It was solid proof that my efforts to change were working. I also admired his affection for a girl who was strange and not particularly pretty. It showed his kindness and depth.

When I saw her the following week, Terri's arm was covered with what appeared to be a cast. Her face wore a permanent look of astonishment, as though she'd survived a war. The unit had looked like its aftermath. Silent questions hovered in the air. I wondered if Lion Boy and I could've intervened. I wondered who was next. But an important shift took place: I stopped dreading these kids. Despite the cruelty some of them had shown Terri, I saw them as broken and scared.

Even in this atmosphere, I was acting more like a regular guy every day. Hope surged through my body. I had a new project—getting emancipated from my parents, having a small apartment in Philadelphia, and completing my schooling there. I overheard kids talking about "emancipation." They told me I'd have the full rights of an adult. That included responsibilities, too, but I could deal with those. Problem was: I'd have to be sixteen, almost a year and a half away. Some states made exceptions. But the idea thrilled me. For the first time, I looked up to older kids as role models. They'd show me how to reconfigure my life.

One of my role models was a twenty-year-old patient. Her wealthy parents kept an apartment for her on posh Rittenhouse Square, in a building whose fifties façade had salmon-colored arabesques. Lit from behind, they looked like eerie smiles. I had seen that building on trips to Philly. She had gone on an extended excursion—a privilege given to patients who were close to getting released. And because she had her own apartment, I thought nothing of her being gone for a month. She didn't even need emancipation; she was old enough to *be* an adult. I hoped to talk to her and get tips. Within two days, I did see her.

The ward door flew open. A gurney wheeled in someone who looked like the Invisible Man, face encased in bandages. A nurse accompanied the patient to her room. I asked another nurse what had happened. She wouldn't say.

At Morning Meeting, we learned the twenty-year-old schizophrenic had gone off her meds and started hearing "voices" again. They told her she had to become a new person by destroying her past identity. The voices convinced her to use a scalding iron to remove all the skin from her face. The notion of creating a new identity sparked empathy in me. But my alteration was about behavior, not flayed flesh. That horrified me. I couldn't get the image out of my mind, picturing hunks of skin attached to the iron.

I asked Cora why the young woman had been brought back to the Toot. The best Cora could figure was she had started to talk again and needed psychiatric care. I asked why the psychiatrist didn't visit her in the physical hospital. Cora shook her head, releasing that *tss* sound people make when they're stumped.

I couldn't get the patient out of my mind, wanting to believe that getting out and living a normal life was within reach. But there was another reason for thinking about her. In the years of taking care of my mother, I realized *I* felt better if I focused on someone else's pain. It diminished my own. I wanted to cheer up the faceless woman.

So I asked the head nurse—we called her "Glasses"— if Terri, Lion Boy, and I could visit the woman in I.C.U. It had to get approved by the shrinks. Finally, an I.C.U. nurse came down to bring us up. This unit was oppressively quiet except for the whirr of air filtration, as though it were breathing for the schizophrenic woman and all of us. It saved us the trouble of finding the right words to say, for it filled up the silence. We approached her bed. The IV drip ticked off seconds with iridescent drops. A red light pulsed behind the bag, giving the solution a sci-fi glow. Although the painkillers had knocked her out, her hands quivered. Staring at the Invisible-Man gauze swathed around her head, I wondered how she breathed. Maybe that's what the air filtration did.

I pictured her inflamed scar tissue below the bandage looking like the arabesques on her building. I worried that when the bandages came off, her features would fuse into a red sneer. I couldn't scrape that image from my mind. However, that's all we ever learned about the woman. Weeks later, orderlies carted her off. We didn't know where.

Uninvited, my old fears cropped up. I worried I would end up like her. I wondered if the crazy-germs from childhood had infected me, after all. My attempt to cheer her up had gone unnoticed. Maybe I could find someone else to help, someone to pour my energies into. There was no shortage of people who needed comforting.

In the Toot, hellish voices lured patients to carve up their bodies and faces. And there I was in the midst of them. I heard no voices. For me, the urge to commit suicide was simple: to extinguish pain. Depression was both the quicksand and the weight pushing me deeper into it. Reaching out to other patients was like trying to grab hold of a tree, to pull myself out. But aside from Terri and Lion Boy, the other patients kept to themselves, or traveled in cliques. Some argued with themselves. Others were bug-eyed, intoxicated—on what, I wasn't sure. My saying "hello" and asking how they were doing jolted them out of their reveries. They smiled, said, "Cool," and kept walking. I felt rejected by these kids at a time when I needed to reach out. I sank into a state so still the word *stillness* can't describe it. That word implies an inner movement, like prayer. This was inertia, an erasure of self.

CHAPTER 14
LESSONS

As if attending a one-room schoolhouse, we had one teacher, Matthew. He knew many of us suffered from depression and said Gerard Manley Hopkins had struggled with it, too. Our teacher asked if the poet chose not to kill himself in "Carrion Comfort." The poem pivoted around the verb "to be." Hopkins wrote, "Not choose not to be."

The students went quiet.

I pointed to another line that describes being gnawed by depression: "Despair not feast on thee." Matthew nodded and asked again about the theme of suicide.

I felt exposed, not wanting it to be common knowledge that I'd tried to hang myself. But after our teacher's question, three other patients admitted to having tried taking their lives. They didn't go into details, and no one pressured them. I saw myself in those students and felt a bond. That never happened before. I wondered if that had been Matthew's intention. Nonetheless, I kept my suicide attempt a secret, having trained myself to be private. I certainly wouldn't mention my new fantasies about cutting my arm, spurred on by patients' actions. But, for the first time in years, I realized I might have friends.

I said even if the poem was about depression and suicide, it wasn't depressing. Ironically, the poem pulsed with life. It brought me into a world I'd never known before, with a language and sounds I couldn't explain but understood. The act of writing had saved the poet. I wanted to invent a language to save *my* life.

Aside from O.T., *this* was the most healing environment at the Toot. This unassuming teacher didn't hold a degree as a therapist. He never wore a suit, but a flannel shirt and baggy corduroy pants, his face framed by a wheat-colored beard, almost covering his mouth. But when he spoke, he lit up. He didn't care that we were teenagers. He discussed literature he loved, showing us new ways of thinking. He'd let us discuss what we thought it meant, not what it *had* to mean. We felt respected.

I asked if it mattered that I didn't always understand poems but loved their music. The way I heard paintings, I also *saw* sounds: burnished, golden, amber. I felt safe enough to mention this "ability" to my classmates. They could have thought I had crazy-germs but instead wanted to hear more. I said I'd studied oil painting. While other art students and I cleaned brushes and palettes, we'd play a game, giving colors to numbers. Most of us agreed that five equaled bright blue; three, yellow. I said symphonies also came alive for me—with colors and contours like three-dimensional paintings. On occasion, I could even smell music. It worked the other way, too. Seeing an abstract composition, I "heard" it in my head, where sight and sound fused.

The kids asked if I had been smoking pot. I said I didn't even smoke cigarettes. My classmates called it "cool," saying they were jealous. One girl, who'd taken LSD, said she'd experienced it then. Matthew called it "synaesthesia," which artists often have. He read an example from Emily Dickinson's poem "I Heard a Fly Buzz—When I Died." She wrote, "With blue—uncertain—stumbling buzz." Matthew explained how she used the visual adjective "blue" to describe a sound. I had never been so honest about this ability and had never felt prouder of it. But I wouldn't tell Archibald. He'd see it as something to correct, something wrong.

I said, "At Group Therapy, we never talk about anything deep. It's usually some jerk ganging up on a kid, and no one stops it." Matthew looked upset.

"Yeah," another boy said. "I'm in a different one, but we never talk about stuff like offing yourself."

Upset by the notion of suicide, Lion Boy said he'd read the Maharishi Mahesh Yogi spoke out against it. He'd been the Beatles' spiritual leader, their guru.

"What's that?" I asked.

"Way more amazing than a priest or a shrink—he can look into your soul."

"What did he say?" I asked.

"If you kill yourself, you get stuck in limbo, with the body's hungers, but no way to satisfy them."

Matthew seemed pleased to have set this discussion in motion but looked at his watch and said we'd continue at our next class. For the first time, I looked forward to meeting with classmates.

Back in my room, I fantasized about a guru who'd tell me, "Of course your fantasies make sense. I speak your language, without words." He would understand me, scanning my thoughts, feelings, talents—even my future—flickering on a magic screen only he could see. I imagined him saying, "I'm watching over you."

The next day, I asked Matthew if I could borrow some

poetry books. He said, "Of course." As I sat reading on the grounds, something touched my arm. A leaf had fallen onto me. Looking up, I remembered seeing my mother walking in the same area. My recollection of her floated toward me like a phantom from seven years earlier. She looked forlorn. I wished I could reach into the past and speak to her with my fourteen-year-old self. I understood what she must have gone through. I tucked the leaf in my pocket, as she had carried my photograph in hers. The memory-ghost vanished.

But I'd have the opportunity to put my new understanding of her to use very soon. My parents were coming the next day. When they showed up, I chose not to tell them about my depressions, the feeling of sinking, and the new thoughts of cutting my arm. Instead, I talked about the books we were reading and the paintings I was doing at O.T. Dad seemed happy to hear about my academic studies but said nothing about my art. He didn't approve of anything he deemed impractical.

More importantly, it was still my duty to protect Mom's happiness. Her eyes moistened. I'd already been at the Toot months longer than she had. A bell rang: only thirty more minutes of visiting time.

To cheer me up, my mother talked about her gourmet club. She knew I had loved eating the leftovers. Every month, a different suburban housewife prepared a lunch in the cuisine of a different culture. The past month had been her turn. She made a Japanese feast, with traditional music and *raku* pottery. She showed me the photographic cookbook, with food made to resemble maple leaves— nothing like the dreary slop at the Toot. The bell rang again: Visiting time was over. I looked down as I hugged Mom. Dad said, "Goodbye, son."

Overcome with feelings I had no words for, I asked the nurse for a pass and went to O.T. I spotted Peggy, braiding gum wrappers. She was a living artifact from my mother's hospitalization. Because Peggy was an adult when I first met her, she seemed to have changed less than I had. And because her lobotomy left her with the mind of a little girl, it's as though she'd grown backward in time. Wearing a cardigan, with flowers stuck in the buttonholes, she had plopped an ill-fitting wig on her head.

"Remember me, Peggy?"

"So many shades of green on holy holly plants tender green thorny garden." Her way of talking started to make sense to me, like poetry. But I was afraid I was the only person who listened to her.

Suddenly, I glanced at my watch; I had to leave for Group Therapy. As much as I loved Matthew's classes and O.T., I hated Group. It was one more "therapeutic" ordeal Archibald had imposed on me. I excused myself to Peggy and darted to the session, which had already begun.

At least Lion Boy was there. Masculine in an unstudied way, he slumped down in his chair as if to say, *I'm not involved in any of this.* He didn't know it, but I had been copying his body language and speech, in my effort to be a "regular guy." Aside from the sexual flush I felt, I liked him as a person. The reason for his hospitalization was he'd shut down, unwilling to go to school or participate in activities. *I'm not involved in any of this* was his response to life.

Neither of us liked Group. Someone was often reduced to tears. That person bolted from the room, slamming the door. This therapy was a process of rasping open emotional scabs until they bled. I never understood the benefit. I was afraid of being verbally attacked. It was only a matter of time before it would be my turn.

But that day, in that windowless, gray-green room, I scored a victory. It involved a bully. He leaned forward, putting people on the defensive. His antagonistic eyes dared, *Yeah, so what of it!* He was attractive, the way a sculpture made of razor blades might be. You'd notice the glitter but wouldn't get close.

After I said that Peggy's way of speaking was beautiful, he asked, "Why don't you say what's on your fuckin' mind?"

"She could use more friends," I said. Looking at him, I realized he was irritated, scratching his arms and legs. I asked, "What's wrong?"

"Just got off the horn with my take-it-up-the-butt dad."

"That's a messed-up thing to say about your father," another kid said.

"I fuckin' hate him," the bully said.

Anyone with father problems piqued my interest, so I asked why.

"No fuckin' balls."

"What?"

"I could make one call and have the old geezer get me outta here."

"Really?"

"Yeah, money equals power. Didn't ya learn that in math class, Suburban Boy?"

"So why not live a normal life?" I said.

"What the fuck's normal?"

"Freedom?"

"Hell, this is fuckin' anarchy boot camp," he said, raising his fist.

A girl who rarely spoke said, "Yeah, and you're Che Guevara."

I added that my family life was so chaotic, all I craved was order.

"Well, relationships are fuckin' complicated," he said.

I told him most kids have mixed feelings toward their parents.

"You've always got generalizations about everything, don't you, Kostos?"

"Sounds like you just made a generalization yourself," I said. It was an obvious, straightforward thing to say, but the entire room—except the bully—broke into laughter that swelled into applause. I had stood up to the one person everyone despised. This triumph gave me a boost of self-esteem—the other patients suddenly liked me. In an environment where I had to go along with everything, this small act of defiance was exciting. The next week, the old dynamics fell into place. The bully was back in charge.

Glasses, the head nurse, was the facilitator. She wore stylish neck-length blonde hair and a miniskirt. Because she wore glossy stockings, her legs reminded me of raw Oscar Mayer hot dogs. She scribbled notes, keeping a cautious distance from this group of primitives. She was like Margaret Mead, and we were Samoans. So as not to disturb our tribal patterns, Glasses didn't get involved, except on rare occasions. Otherwise, she treated us with indifference. Her apathy gave rise to some of the crueler taunts. Most of these patients never came to Matthew's classes. If they did, they acted differently there. Like the bully I stood up to, many of the kids enjoyed confrontations.

To a pregnant girl, they said, "Too bad your mom's gotta take care of that baby you were stupid enough to have. Time to get your tubes tied." Or, "Hey, Terri, since you cut up your right arm, why not be symmetrical and do the left one?" These kids never tormented her if Lion Boy was there. I kept practicing his fuck-you slump, which became my default body language. I was putting on regular-guy airs. Even so, I still guarded myself. These kids were talented at sniffing out vulnerabilities.

The most frequent target was Terri. Her trail of blood had initiated me onto the ward. Yet she managed to snare gorgeous Lion Boy. I felt jealous but never told her. She mothered him while he pretended not to care. No one dared hassle *him*. I was learning from that example. *A regular guy never gets bullied.* If I kept at it, my new Dean was within reach.

But when Lion Boy was absent (which he was half the time), Terri protested some cruel statement, racing through the hall, mascara bleeding. We were left in the suffocating room for the remaining half hour, unwilling to speak. I remained in that fuck-you position, feeling guilty for not having stood up for her. The bully I'd confronted found her outbreaks funny. Glasses kept scrawling. I was convinced she would've kept taking notes even if a patient had stabbed another one. We were just clinical subjects.

I asked Dr. Archibald to let me out of Group, the way I had pleaded to stay on the adult ward, the way I had begged not to go to Bakely. The more I did so, the more he used the word "therapeutic." He was of the if-the-medicine-tastes-awful-it-must-be-good-for-you school of thought. I knew its tenets. My father had graduated cum laude from that university. I tried a different strategy the next time I met with Archibald:

"Ya think cruelty helps people grow?" I asked.

"Why?"

"That's what always happens in Group."

"Shouldn't we address how that makes you feel?"

I sat there, glaring at him, waiting for him to say something kind, maybe an apology. But as he stared back, I got angrier. It intensified as it had when I'd fought that bully in the snow. I went blank again. What else could I do? Archibald's Thai trash can was close to me, so I lifted it up and heaved it at him, papers flying onto both of us. The trash can missed him.

Then he did what he was born to do with those ridiculously large, flashing teeth—he laughed as if he'd heard a joke at a garden party. It showed he wasn't bothered by me at all. I was a minor annoyance. If I got angrier, he'd simply find that funny, too.

Realizing I couldn't win, I felt diminished. And from some old code that a bullied kid never forgets, I gave in, the way a defeated country gives in to its conqueror. I sat there, seething *and* embarrassed. But I had another strategy. I would study *him*, as he'd been studying me. If I could make sense of him, maybe I could figure out my father.

"Feel better?" he said.

I shrugged.

"Were you hoping to knock me out?" He chuckled again. "Sons do fantasize about murdering their fathers— it's Oedipal."

"Edible?" I asked.

"No, from Oedipus, the Greek king who killed his father."

Sometimes I wished Dad would die, especially when he mocked me. I told Archibald, "My art teacher filled a pitcher with flowers for us to paint with watercolor."

"Does that have something to do with your father?"

"Yes. Archery."

"What?"

"I brought my painting home to show Mom. She loved it."

Archibald picked up more papers, throwing them into his dented trash can.

"Then I showed the painting to Dad, who was giving Phil archery lessons. Laughing, my father said the painting looked like piss on paper."

"Why didn't you get angry at him the way you just got angry at me?"

Instead of saying that would've been impossible, I told him a nearby town had art competitions for adults and kids. My watercolor won second place in the adult contest.

"How did that make you feel?"

"Proud, but it never took the hurt away," I said. Dad later asked Phil to go to a ballgame, looking straight through me. I sneaked into the garage, where my father kept his 1954 MG. Its leather seats smelled of his pipe tobacco. Inside the car, feeling close to him, I cried myself to sleep.

Because I had a lousy relationship with my father, Archibald explained that another male role model would help. I was going to work with a resident, Dr. Mandrill. Archibald never explained how an additional shrink would do me any good. I figured I was to be observed like a monkey in a cage by a man furthering his studies. Like Group, I had no choice. I looked out the window when I felt overwhelmed.

There, Peggy came into view, trespassing in the azalea gardens. She started attaching plastic flowers to the bushes. Two orderlies spotted her. They tried lifting her up from her armpits. As she squirmed, one of the men fell into the thicket. He rose up scratched, but triumphant, clasping her arm. She was bleeding and crying.

Sliding his cuff from his watch, Archibald said, "Time's up."

I stomped back to the ward, annoyed about Peggy's defeat, annoyed I had exposed my feelings to someone who didn't give a shit. Alone in my room, I blasted "Light My Fire" by the Doors. I allowed myself to "see" the sounds, drawing with India ink on watercolor paper. I drew roots tangling into the earth, eye-shaped seeds fallen from trees. My pen snagged on the paper's grain, ink splattering onto the landscape. Instead of being discouraged, I crosshatched the error until another form rose up. I thought the mistake had happened to inspire me. Maybe I could use Group and working with the new resident the same way. What seemed like a mistake could strengthen my transformation into a regular guy. I would be my own creation, my own drawing. I trusted my pen. The strokes became a trunk, branches—a tree. It curved into the empty side of the drawing. My love of art, synaesthesia, and Matthew's lessons were helping. I wasn't powerless anymore.

CHAPTER 15
HOMO GEIGER COUNTER

Dr. Mandrill showed up at my door after O.T. He had black, slicked-back hair, dark eyes, and a cleft chin. I couldn't stop thinking about the monkey with his name, the one that sticks out its butt. The resident's first visit was an introduction, and because it was on my turf, I felt in control. I told him I'd slept poorly and needed to nap. He said he'd show up from "time to time."

Unlike Archibald, Mandrill would go on visiting my room without advance notice. "Just dropping by," he'd say, but I knew it wasn't random. I sat on my bed, and there he was across from me—too intimate—in his black suit, white shirt, and narrow tie, always loosened. He crossed his legs and peered into me. I felt invaded. By the second visit, he already brought up sex. I'm not sure what provoked it. He didn't need a push.

I said, "Sometimes I can't concentrate."

"Well, you need concentration to do anything, even to have sex."

"Really? I thought it was supposed to be fun."

"Oh, it *is*." Then he proceeded to tell me things he did with his wife, ending with, "But you'd have to ask *her* about that."

Why on earth did he think I cared? Maybe it was only a ruse to smoke me out. Maybe his sexy eyes could see the images I summoned when I played with myself. I imagined the resident sitting there with some kind of homo Geiger counter, calibrating my desires.

I became stone-faced. Every time he made a comment

like, "My tongue can sure make my wife happy," I shut down a bit more. Was all that nattering about his wife just a scheme to make me want him? Unfortunately, Mandrill's and Archibald's comments succeeded in making me feel dirty. No, dirtier.

Sitting on the edge of my bed, I told him about having gone on my first excursion in seven months—to the Philadelphia Zoo. We'd seen a Mandrill monkey parading with its butt in the air. I said it looked like him. I'd get to him by teasing.

In truth, I was afraid he knew me better than I did. Increasingly, sexual fantasies filled my thoughts. I kept having the same dream, one I never told either shrink about: I entered a long, shadowy corridor lit by red bulbs. Moving forward in slow motion, I passed rows of shirtless youths, my age and older—maybe two hundred of them. They stood along the entire length of the hall. With no words spoken, no eye contact made, I walked forward. As I did, the young men start lowering their jeans in unison, inch by inch. I never saw them pull their pants all the way down. Just before they did, the dream went dark—my sheets wet. I woke up.

"So why are you telling me about that monkey? Because of my name?"

"I guess."

"You made a point of talking about his butt. Is *that* what you want to tell me?"

"I'm no fag."

"That's a rather strong reaction."

I wouldn't let him pry further, had to shut him up. "I'm asexual, if you must know. Feel better now?"

He gave me a smug, amused look and said he had rounds to make. I was delighted to get him off my back.

Although the Toot officially condemned it, sexual activity was rampant on our ward. Friends said Terri and Lion Boy did it when the half-deaf nurse was on duty.

When Terri and I sat together, she showed a different side, "I ain't foolin' myself—what I got with Lion's a fling. I mean, look at me."

"Like you don't deserve him?" I asked. I was enjoying him vicariously through her. We both felt undeserving. If I could cure her of those feelings, maybe I'd heal my own. What she wanted, I wanted. I could never tell anyone that—least of all Terri. But I could be her confidant, as I had been Mom's.

"No, Sweetie," she said. "I'm realistic. If some pretty girl slithers into this snake pit, she'll get all his attention."

"Won't that piss you off?"

"Hell, I'd be fuckin' happy for him. No guy stays with me."

"Would you still be ... friends?"

"Maybe, but I ain't no angel—if some cute guy shows up on wacko ward. . . ."

I looked up, confused. "Oh," I managed to say. What would it be like if she ditched Lion Boy, and he wanted *me*? I closed my eyes and pictured myself in his arms.

"See—we're alike, me and Lion," Terri said.

At that moment, she saw him on the grounds. She banged on the window, gesturing for him to wait. I watched the two of them stroll arm-in-arm on the lawn. Shirtless, he looked like one of the boys in my dream. No, I wasn't asexual, but I didn't feel safe telling anyone

111

about my desires. I either stuffed them inside or railed about how disgusting faggots were, knowing I was one—the part of me I hadn't managed to kill.

As predicted, Lion Boy's affections would soon turn to a new patient, a girl with a mysterious name—Chambliss. She entered the unit more as an atmosphere than a person. Chambliss was an old family name, she later told me. A bookish young woman, eyes the color of old pennies, she divulged no secrets. She brought mystery and class to the ward.

Since she arrived two days before my fifteenth birthday, I invited her to my party in the lunchroom. Cora had decorated it with yellow balloons. And because chocolate sandwiches were my favorite snack, she'd gotten the kitchen staff to make ten of them—bittersweet chocolate, melted between slabs of French bread. I was amazed they gave in to this extravagance. Everyone at the party got one. My chocolate sandwich had a candle pierced through the middle. I focused on its flame as Cora, Matthew, my new friends from Unit I, and even Peggy (a nurse had escorted her) sang "Happy Birthday." I was disappointed the sad man hadn't come. And although turning fifteen in a loony bin didn't seem to warrant the word "happy," I smiled and blew out the candle. Then I gave it a second thought. Surrounded by people who liked me and had no intention of tormenting me, I *was* happier than I'd been in a long time. Though I initially dreaded Unit I, it was infinitely better than school back home or Bakely Academy. A mental hospital wasn't where I'd hoped to end up, but it turned out to be a place where I could grow. Friends, old and new, were helping to make that happen.

I immediately sensed Chambliss and I could become close. So, when she wasn't with Lion Boy, I approached her, finding her a good listener. I learned she loved poetry and wrote it regularly. That was the beginning of our poetry-writing dialogue, continuing for almost a year and a half. We recast our angers, hurts, and fears into stanzas. And even though I was afraid Lion might think I was "interested" in her, he quickly saw our relationship was platonic. He'd even join our poetry sessions.

But I didn't show her my poems until I developed them first, afraid they weren't good enough. After revisions, I read what I still considered rough drafts to Cora. She appreciated the images, but was quick to notice if it didn't sound like me. She wanted the poems to be "honest." To be sure, I'd become guarded with most people—even myself. But Cora's coaxing allowed me to be less afraid. I'd show the next version to Chambliss, who'd give me suggestions on how to polish it further. Eventually, I had a great idea—I asked Cora if the Toot might be interested in starting a poetry magazine, with work written by patients. While she loved the idea, she couldn't get the administrators to take it seriously. Even so, I kept showing her my poems, which I stored in a brown grocery bag.

Sometimes, waiting for Cora at the nurse's station, I'd have to take off, finding a patient had become violent. It was usually over not wanting to take antipsychotic meds. I'd heard kids' complaints in the Day Room and at Group. Their side effects ranged from dizziness and dry mouth to rashes and nausea—even headaches and tremors. They said the reactions were worse than the disorders.

But I knew how adamant the nurses were about meds. They'd stand by each patient, who had to stick his or her tongue out, to show the pill had been swallowed. The staff preferred liquid meds—less easily spat out.

No one forced me to take antidepressants. However, on occasion, I asked Archibald to prescribe Valium, to take the edge off my anxiety, helping me to sleep. Because it was addictive, I couldn't take it too often.

That was nothing compared to what these kids endured. They took pills that made them sick and unable to function. It seemed like the cruelest form of domination. The patient would growl at the nurses who forced the meds, "Get the fuck off me, you mother fuckin' fascists!" I didn't blame the kid for getting angry. I felt angry, too. Nonetheless, I'd hightail it back to my room, hearing chairs slammed, glass breaking. In minutes, orderlies—squat, muscular men with expressionless faces—subdued the schizophrenic kid. Thrashing him or her to the floor, they'd use a straitjacket, as if trussing a chicken. One of the prim, self-righteous nurses would then inject Thorazine, Haldol, or something that induced a stupor.

Because I'd seen it many times, I could picture it from my room. It had never happened to me. I swore it never would. Being assaulted before gawking patients would be more than I could forgive the Toot or myself for. That, above all else, would have pushed me to take my life. Instead of listening to my beloved radio, I walked to the turntable, swung the arm back, playing a 45 of "Eleanor Rigby." I let it repeat over and over—for at least an hour—to drown out the thud of defeat, to remind me of the vow I'd taken with a noose around my neck.

Chapter 16
Displacements

I took a shortcut to Archibald's office through a maze of underground tunnels—a subterranean world that linked the buildings. Turning the corner, I doubled up the stairs and was about to knock on his door. Instead, he opened it. "We're in sync, both a few minutes early," Archibald said.

As I eased into the leather chair, I looked onto the grounds, saying I sometimes pictured Mom there as a patient. That opened a discussion about how the past never goes away, but each person's memory of it varies. He confirmed that family members often recall the same incident differently.

"When I tell you stuff that happened, I'm not sure my details are right," I said.

"What you *do* remember will reveal a lot."

I told him Mom had shared family stories for years—a kind of memory heirloom. The anecdotes involved my grandmother, *Yiayá*. She'd met her husband in Greece, before World War I. He dreamed of being a chiropractor. In America, doctors could choose not to fight if they provided medical service. After coming to New York, he earned a scholarship to NYU. My grandmother supported him, sewing for a furrier. They had a daughter but couldn't afford more kids till he earned his degree. In fact, they were so broke they sent her to live with his family in Athens.

"The way *you* were sent away?" Archibald asked.

"Come to think of it, yes." Hesitating, I explained how every time my grandfather got *Yiayá* pregnant, he rigged a leather harness around her hips and tied it to a detached potbelly stove. He made her drag it through the apartment till she miscarried. I'd heard this from my mother, who hadn't been born yet. She said my grandmother bled terribly, suffering excruciating pain and guilt.

"Guilt because of her religious beliefs?"

"Probably, but the Church doesn't approve of psychics either."

"Psychics?"

A coworker told my grandmother about a clairvoyant, who predicted this baby would be a boy. My grandfather wouldn't make his wife get rid of a male fetus. It dawned on me that my family had followed these old-world hierarchies: Phil was the boy. I didn't have to tell anyone I was a daughter in a son's body. They'd always treated me that way.

"What happened?" Archibald asked.

"My grandfather let her have the baby. Instead of a boy, he got a girl—my mother." And he doted on her. Their financial situation improved after he graduated. But he started complaining of chest pains. As a chiropractor, he wouldn't even take aspirin.

One day, after *Yiayá* left to deliver satin linings, my mother heard her father fall in the bathroom. He groaned, pushed open the door, and died in her arms like a strange pietà. She was six.

No longer obligated to my grandfather, relatives in Greece wanted his first daughter to join her mother.

But the girl didn't know her younger sister, and the father she barely knew had just died. Nonetheless, my mother's sister was sent back to New York. One night, my grandmother invited American relatives for dessert. After they left, Mom and *Yiayá* cleaned up. My grandmother sighed, wishing her husband were there. That triggered the older daughter, Mary. Like poison erupting from a broken ampoule, she snapped. Shoving the tray from her mother's hands, she punched the woman, who fell to the floor. Careful not to bruise her face, the girl pummeled her mother in the head.

"What did your grandmother do?" Archibald asked.

"Pleaded for her not to hurt her younger sister," I said. "Then *Yiayá* did something weird—she begged for more."

"Why?" he asked.

"To atone for the abortions."

"Do you make *yourself* suffer for your guilt?" I felt punched in the stomach by his question. But he was right: guilt for my parents' screwed up marriage? Yep. For Phil's behavior? Yep. For being a fag? I pushed that disgusting word out of my mind. Gathering my thoughts, I said that despite *Yiayá's* pleas, the girl bashed her younger sister unconscious for "killing" their father. That was the start of beatings that continued for years.

"Does that strike a chord?"

"You mean the bullies?"

"Yes."

I looked up at him, again surprised by his understanding.

"There's displacement in your family," he said.

"Dis-what?"

"Your aunt took out her anger on people who didn't hurt her."

"Oh, I get it—easy targets." I'd worn a bull's-eye most of my life.

"Something like that," he said.

I told him how Mom waited after school in the library. At six o'clock, she'd meet her mother on the corner to head up to the apartment. Together, they'd survive my aunt's attacks. Alone, they were afraid she'd kill them.

"Like you were afraid Phil would shoot *you*?"

"I guess." I told him Mom was trapped, till she was thirteen. Bigger then, she snuck up from behind and flipped her sister onto the floor. My mother squatted on her chest, slammed *her* head, and screamed the beatings had to stop. Her older sister never laid a hand on my mother or *Yiayá* again.

Years later, when I told Mom about being bullied, she taught me how to fight. Archibald said usually a father would have done that. My mother, while fragile at times, had a tough side. I respected that.

He then returned to the topic of the past, how it shapes the present, asking if I had other remembrances. I recounted darting across our backyard and swinging from a tree. I felt a tug, looked up, and saw Mom framed by the kitchen window. She stood there, losing herself in me and the green world I claimed. Showing off, I dangled from the branch like an acrobat. Her glance flew out to me, and I caught it with my own, as a trapeze artist catches his partner midair.

"Your alliance with your mother was important."

I agreed and described how I pored over her photo

album, to *see* her past. We were in the kitchen, where I often helped prepare dinner. Dad, she complained, was too busy for her with his law practice, his position as mayor, *and* his pro bono work."

Archibald asked, "What kind?"

"For the Civil Rights movement."

"Why?"

I said he took pride in telling me a Greek-Orthodox archbishop was the first white cleric to march with Martin Luther King. I assumed Dad had strong feelings about that because his parents had lived as second-class citizens and then as refugees. He was raised in East Harlem.

"So, there's a compassionate side to your father?"

"Yeah. It's confusing." I described turning to a photograph where someone had been torn away. My mother walked to the sink, saying she didn't want her photo album ruined by someone cruel. The person replaced by a jagged halo was her sister, Maria or Mary.

Archibald explained how people who've been hurt need to express their anger, in order to heal. He looked at me intently. I knew he remembered my heaving a trash can at him, not that I meant to hit him. But I *was* expressing my anger as my mother had shown hers, which probably saved her life. I figured this was Archibald's way of saying he understood and respected me. I wanted to believe that.

Chapter 17
Visitations

Mom tilted her head into my hospital room, a smile spreading across her face. Because Archibald wasn't around, she and Dad would spend their entire visit with me. She beamed, announcing they'd gotten permission to take me on a day excursion. With a laminated pass from the nurse's station, I followed my parents out the ward, into their car, and away from the Toot. They were so nice to each other and me I started wondering if I'd made their fights up.

They asked where I wanted to go. I said I'd heard about the trendy shops on Samson Street. As if my wishes suddenly mattered, my parents took me shopping for clothes—the kind normal teens wore on TV. Mom and Dad waited as I tried on shirts and bellbottoms. These outfits were like costumes: I could pretend I *was* a normal kid. I even caught glimpses of myself in the mirror and thought I looked good. Usually I cringed at my image in reflections or photographs, seeing myself as deformed. I wasn't sure where this positive new way of seeing came from. It was as if I'd temporarily stepped through a door into a brighter room; I wanted it to last. Almost giddy, I asked if we could go to the nearby record store. Mom said, "Of course." Walking into the shop, I eyed row after row of albums: all the music I'd been hearing on the radio. Customers tapped their feet, listening to records with earphones. I lost myself in this buffet of music, and my parents didn't rush me. I finally chose The Beatles' *The White Album*.

Hungry, we had lunch at a French bistro specializing in crepes, which reminded me of Zili's café. As I reminisced about that magical night, Mom lowered her voice, reminding me we had to go back to the Toot. The drive to West Philly was silent. I had so many conflicting emotions. I wasn't sure what to say, or how to say it. I wanted to tell them I missed them and my old life. But what sense would that make? That life hadn't been so great. I was longing for something that never existed: a family to make me feel safe. After our car passed through the entrance to the stone wall, I thanked them, muttering, "I love you." Wearing clothes from the outside world, I felt like an impostor; I was no longer of that world. I disappeared into the Toot without turning around. I knew Mom and Dad would be back in a week.

Until then, I followed the scheduled cycle of therapy, Morning Meetings, Matthew's classes, O.T., and Group. However, when my parents came the next time, they didn't take me on an excursion. We spent the visit walking the hallways and grounds. I said I'd love to go for a drive. But no—Archibald meted out excursions stingily. Mom said it was pleasant just getting to know each other better. And our visit was enjoyable, at first. Although they were sweet and affectionate at first, she and Dad started growling insults at each other. I didn't understand what set them off. Whatever depression I'd been slogging through turned to tar; I couldn't move. Having slept poorly the night before, I said I needed to nap. That got rid of them for the time being. But the Toot loved schedules, so I'd see them every week, barring Dad's business trips.

When they visited the following week, they spent only fifteen minutes with me. Mom brought my favorite candy, Rolo, like an apology, and headed off to meet with Archibald. A devotee of the psychiatric faith, she saw him as the secular equivalent of an archbishop. I never learned what they had decided in those sessions. But afterward, my parents had annoyingly fake smiles, treating me like a stranger. I figured it was based on something Archibald said. But at least they weren't fighting—I welcomed peace in whatever form it took.

The worst type of visit was for "family sessions." These were pure hell—worse than Group, worse than sitting through Mom and Dad's arguments alone. They got to hurl barb after vicious barb before Dr. Archibald (and me). Phil was lucky; he never came. But I had to sit through this torture for my "well-being."

Mom needled Dad, complaining how stubborn he was—ignorant of psychological theories, with no interest in learning. He was too "narcissistic," a word she emphasized. "Surprising for such an educated man, a lawyer." She then explained how she'd driven to Philadelphia one night a week to study Political Science. When she tried discussing world events with my father, he said she had no business yammering about things she didn't understand. I was angry at Dad but kept quiet.

Barely letting the words escape from clenched teeth, he said, "Sofia, that's enough yappin', damn it." I associated that verb with a small, irritating dog. It was his way of calling her a bitch. But my lawyer father had a vast vocabulary. When I used to read in the rec room, instead of looking up a word, I just asked him. He always knew what it meant, how to spell it, even its language of origin. However, when he got mad, he became that boy from the streets again. His vocabulary changed. "Yappin'" was one of those words. It made him seem tough. It was also a warning, one Mom never heeded.

Expecting Dr. Archibald to take her side, she looked at him with a conspiratorial smile and continued to goad Dad. I'd seen her do it before. I'd even been on the receiving end of her verbal attacks. In those moments, some weird force took over her, raging out of control. Everyone in her path stopped talking, afraid of inciting her further. Wanting to intervene, I was too terrified. Afterward, she'd be fine—even jovial, as if nothing had happened. But I felt flayed alive.

Usually, when my parents lost their tempers, my dissociation kicked in. I blanked out, the way everything goes white when you fly above a certain altitude. I couldn't recall one word of their squabble. But on this day, I *did* remember. She kept looking to Dr. Archibald, expecting him to chime in and take her side. He just sat there, coolly observing all three of us. His entertainment. It's what people do to caged animals. I resented it and squeezed my hands until they turned red. Dad had enough of her insults and stormed out. I wished I could have done the same but wasn't allowed.

Pleased with herself, Mom turned to Archibald, "Typical. But what can you expect of a narcissist?" She awaited his reply, certain he'd finally take her side. He said nothing, hoping she'd keep speaking. Flustered at his lack of support, she stomped out, too.

There I was, alone with him. I said, "You see why I can't get along with Dad?"

"Given your mother's provocations, I was impressed by his self-control."

"His what?"

"Some men would have responded by hitting her. Your father had the wisdom to remove himself before—"

"Really?"

"Your mother was almost inviting it ... what she learned from her sister."

I had never taken Dad's side before, but what Archibald said made more sense than I wanted to admit. I told him I still hoped to reunite them, as I had when I was a boy. Back then, I tried defusing their arguments with my laughter. Mom said it should've been bottled to make sick people well. But it stopped working. When Dad hightailed it to the municipal building—to escape the marriage and us—I used another strategy. Mom would ask me to walk there, to cajole him to join us for dinner. Had she called, the secretary would've said he was out. They wouldn't treat a little boy that way. I knew a shortcut up the hill. When I reached the building, a man let me in. I then told Dad that Mom had made dinner and wanted him to eat with us. His face drooped as if it were melting. We took the MG back home, roof down, my bangs blowing in the wind.

"How did your parents react to each other?"

"They hugged like it hurt."

"You worked so hard as a boy."

"But Dad seemed ... humiliated."

Archibald told me I needed to stop blaming myself for the state of their marriage. I said I felt guilty about Phil, too. Before my hospitalization, he drowned himself in booze and drugs. I asked if maybe *I* was evil, causing everyone's misery.

Saddened, Archibald shook his head. "I'd like you to try some homework," he suggested. My parents were coming to celebrate Thanksgiving. I was to be conscious of my behavior. If I felt the need to smooth things over, I had to "detach." That would help me to stop holding myself responsible for their fights. I wondered if this assignment would speed my transformation into someone who deserved happiness. Thanking Archibald, I padded out the door.

Chapter 18
Puerto Rico

"Your parents are here," Cora said, rapping on my door.

"Tell them to meet me in the Day Room." I threw on fresh clothes and hoofed it down the hall.

"Happy Thanksgiving, Son," Dad said. He rarely called me by my name, addressing me like a juror with his lawyer voice. I asked where my brother was. Mom smiled nervously. Phil—my father explained—had been enrolled in a military school. It offered a disciplined environment and a fine education. He said they could even enroll me, after the Toot. I sighed, wondering if he'd forgotten what a nightmare boarding school had been. Seeing the alarm on my face *and* my mother's, he added he simply wanted to offer me the same opportunities.

I redirected the conversation, saying I'd gotten the results of my IQ test.

"Dr. Archibald informed us," Dad said. "Smart enough to be a lawyer."

He seemed intent on molding me into a version of himself. I countered, "Wanna see stuff I've been doing at O.T.?"

"Maybe later," he said.

Mom was silent. I thought for sure *she* would have shown interest in my artwork. Instead, she said, "Sweetheart, we have a surprise. Come with us."

I followed her to the end of the ward, where they'd pushed two card tables together and dressed them with a cloth. Mom had made a full Thanksgiving dinner, arranging the turkey, side dishes, and place settings around a centerpiece of chrysanthemums. Dad carved the turkey as if performing an autopsy. He and Mom tried to make small talk, as though they were afraid of upsetting me. Whether it was in response to something Archibald said or an epiphany they reached on their own, I was relieved. Mom handed me a plate of food. "Sonshine, it's hot," she said.

Because they seemed more agreeable than usual, I asked, "Are you guys together again?" She said they had been on the brink of divorce, but a new marriage counselor had helped them to communicate better. With the insights and tools he'd given them, they renewed a commitment to healing their marriage.

"That's great," I said.

"Yes, honey, it is," she said. Dad smiled.

I felt like I hadn't heard the whole story, the way I only caught snippets of my mother's conversations when she spoke to my grandmother in Greek. But I tried to be happy for them. Our chatter dissolved into quiet chewing. In that moment, something peaceful about being together filled me: I was content.

When Dad got up to use the restroom, I said to Mom, "Only one thing would make this better."

"What's that?"

"If Phil was here."

She said I wasn't supposed to know, but he'd been expelled from the military school. She wouldn't say why. It was so upsetting to my father, I had to swear I'd never tell him she told me. While I appreciated her honesty, it underscored the old alliances: Phil and Dad, Mom and me. Our partnership was still the powerless one. She even stood up for my father, saying he hadn't really lied; he was just having a hard time accepting Phil's expulsion. Their counselor called it "denial."

I assumed my brother had chosen not to visit me out of embarrassment. Admitting that was true, Mom also wanted me to know he loved me. She confided that after my commitment, he'd slept with my T-shirt under his pillow for a week. She found it making his bed. My hospitalization had disturbed Phil so much he wouldn't talk about it. Fighting the conflicted feelings I had for him, I wondered if I'd ever understood him, or even could. The way my parents were working on their reconciliation, I could patch my relationship with my brother—maybe when I'd see him for Christmas.

It was getting dark. I told my parents to head home to avoid holiday traffic. They passed through the door with the safety-glass window, and I waved until they vanished. I stayed in my room till morning.

After breakfast, Cora found a way to cheer me up. "Look—doves and invisible thread. Let's decorate for Christmas."

"Got any other stuff?"

"A tree and two whole boxes I brought from home."

As I began hanging garlands, Chambliss, Terri, and some new patients joined me. We worked till Cora's shift ended.

"Don't worry, Cora, we'll finish up," I said. Although other patients lost interest, Chambliss kept working with me. Even professionally decorated trees couldn't compare with ours. A flock of doves hovered above it, moved by whirring vents. After midnight, I traipsed back to my room, proud of what Chambliss and I created.

The next day, Cora claimed the decorations were better than she could've imagined. I beamed. Then she said my parents had good news, but I'd have to wait for them to tell me.

Two days later, Dad whistled "Dearly Beloved" down the hall—a watery, flute-like sound. Mom told me they'd made plans for a family vacation, to help us "bond." Because I'd been doing everything the staff and Archibald asked, and because I hadn't talked about suicide for months, I got excursion rights.

Later that day, we headed to a family session. It proceeded without even a hint of cruelty or drama. I imagined my efforts to get Mom and Dad to fall in love again were paying off.

"Promise me you'll stay with your parents," Archibald said at the end of the session.

"Sure thing," I said, thinking this romantic trip would finally reunite them. But I wouldn't tell him that and risk his mockery.

Destination: Puerto Rico. Exotic to a boy who'd grown up in South Jersey. I'd not only get out of the Toot, but *far* away. The next two weeks dragged until departure. On the second week of December, my parents, Phil, and I flew to New York. From there, Puerto Rico. It was barely ten degrees in New York, but in Puerto Rico, it was a breezy seventy-five. We carried our scratchy, woolen coats off the plane. We piled into a cab, whisked to the hotel. I saw the gleaming marble building and fountains spewing lit waters. Poinsettias lined the pathways.

My brother looked irritated. I'd share a room with him, my parents in a separate one. Given Phil's and my troubled histories, it seemed unwise to put us together— another example of Dad's "denial." I assumed my parents had worked out these arrangements with Archibald. But this plan made no sense, and it worried me more than I wanted to admit. To make matters worse, I was scared of acting like a mental patient.

I silenced these fears by reasoning this trip would be the perfect opportunity for two reconciliations: parents and brothers. Besides, I was thrilled to have this degree of freedom.

An hour after we checked into our rooms and unpacked our bags, I heard a knock on the door: Mom spoke through the wood, "Boys, we'll meet in the lobby at six. We're going somewhere with outdoor dining."

"Wow, eating outdoors in December!" I said.

"I feel kinda lousy," my brother mumbled.

I opened the door and let Mom in. She said, "I was hoping we'd *all* be together."

"I wouldn't be good company," he said.

"Are you sick?" she asked.

"Maybe it was that crappy airplane food."

"I feel terrible, Sweetheart, but if you're sure. . . ."

"Yeah," he said. "I gotta lay down."

"Mom, I'll take care of him," I said. "I'll meet you and Dad in the lobby."

I pressed the door closed. Phil seemed mad. He didn't talk, rolling away from me in his twin bed. I believed we all had to be together, for the sake of our parents' marriage. My brother was foiling the plans, but nothing

130

I said convinced him to join us. I didn't believe he was sick. He'd acted that way when I'd tried talking about The Gun. Surely my parents knew about his drinking and drugging. It was reckless to leave him alone. But when it came to Phil, Dad's rules disregarded logic.

Just the same, I prepared to go out with my parents. My hair had grown long while I'd been at the Toot. I slicked it into a pony tail, changed into a navy-blue blazer, and zoomed downstairs. In the center of the lobby, surrounded by palms, a parrot perched in an antique cage. Her name was Rosalinda. I practiced my junior-high Spanish with her, waiting for my parents.

They stepped from the elevator—as dressed up as when they had attended political soirées. Dad whistled "Dearly Beloved," holding Mom's hand.

I introduced them to my new Spanish-speaking friend. *"Rosalinda, buenas noches."*

"Buenas noches," Rosalinda squawked.

As my parents laughed, we left the lobby, strolled along palm-lined avenues, and arrived at a restaurant with an outdoor garden. Lanterns glowed overhead. Having ordered lobster, I found the green liquid part disgusting. I made my parents laugh, calling it "fly juice." But I forgot about that as soon as dessert arrived— flambé! Its flickering light shone on the waiter's face. The outer shell of the desert was deep-fried dough; the core, dark-chocolate ice cream. I closed my eyes, savoring it. The feeling of contentment returned. The Toot seemed a reality away. I even let go of my anxiety about Phil. *This* was what I wanted. Mom and Dad were together again. It was as if, in flying far away, we'd left both winter and anger behind. I pretended I wasn't a suicidal boy on an excursion from a mental hospital, but a normal kid with parents who loved each other, and a big brother who took care of me. On this tropical island, we could recreate ourselves. Archibald called this "magical thinking," but evidence of it was unfolding before me.

On the way back to the hotel, we passed rows of flame trees. My father picked a red flower and tucked it into my mother's dark hair. He then used the nickname I hadn't heard for years, "Sudsy, sometimes I forget how beautiful you are." She smiled. The fiery flower seemed to wield a spell. Pressing close to each other, my parents held hands as we walked back to the hotel.

Past the poinsettias, into the lobby, past Rosalinda, up the elevator, a hug and kiss from Mom and Dad, a left turn to my room. Dreading what I might find there, I assured myself, *Everything's getting better.* Opening the door, I saw my brother still in bed, his back to me. I thought he was sleeping. But as I got closer, I heard moaning. My heart raced. I thought someone had hurt him, or he was seriously ill. Almost delirious, he rolled over to me, the whites of his eyes showing, his tongue lolling from his mouth, vomit splattered on his shirt.

Overwhelmed by fear, I stuttered, "Wh-what?" I didn't want to look any closer but had to. There it was, stuck in his arm: a syringe. I couldn't catch my breath. An empty vial sat on the nightstand, the floor and comforter splashed with puke. Its odor seemed to expand, crawling into my nostrils.

"Wh-what happened?" I asked.

"You gotta help me," he said.

"Who did this?"

"Shut the hell up and listen. You gotta promise you'll never tell. I mean *never*."

"Why?"

"'Cause I could get locked up for a long time for this shit. And it would be *your* fuckin' fault."

"Why's that in your arm?"

"Get a wet washcloth and stop asking questions."

I wanted nothing more than to run screaming down the hall, summon the police, and wake my parents but couldn't. Fear, anger, and blame gnarled inside me. Unable to think, I drenched a washcloth, bringing it to him.

He'd already taken the needle out. I didn't see where he'd put it. On the nightstand, something lay under a rumpled T-shirt. Phil had owned that stupid firearm— symbol of everything that went wrong with our family— but never did anything violent with it. I reasoned with myself that he couldn't have possibly gotten it on the plane. I didn't lift the shirt to see if it was The Gun, for fear of retaliation. Better not to know. If I saw it, I'd have to tell my parents and the police.

Numb, I cleaned up the puke, ignored its acrid stink, and rinsed washcloths. When I got back from the bathroom, he'd hidden the syringe and what seemed to be The Gun. I pleaded with him to let me call a doctor. He warned if I did, I wouldn't see my next birthday.

Panicked that he'd die or shoot me, I waited till he rolled away from me and darted out the room. I had no one to help me. The image of him imprinted itself on my eyes. Alone with this secret, I sank into depression.

To fight it, I scurried down to the lobby to find Rosalinda, but someone had covered her cage with a cloth. I chatted with the concierge instead. He couldn't possibly imagine what had just happened in my room, or where I'd go after my vacation. He was a student, with relatives in the Bronx, and dreamt of going to college in New York City. It was exciting, we agreed. He was cheerful and optimistic; I wished I could be him.

The poinsettias outside the window seemed to emit a blood-colored light. As I stared at them, I agonized that my brother might have gotten worse. Or died. Fear and dread were like evil spirits. When I denied their existence, they lunged back with a vengeance. I gave into them like appeasing some god who thrives on beating hearts, wrenched from sacrificial victims. I'd allow myself to be sacrificed if it meant things would improve. But I knew better. The lanterns, the flame tree, the possibility of a happy family evaporated.

I feigned a yawn and said goodnight to the concierge, returning with foreboding to the room. It still reeked of vomit. I pictured Phil as a corpse, ashen-white and cold. Hearing him breathe, I was relieved and pulled back the crisp covers of my bed. Terrified I'd wake to find him dead, I tossed for an hour and fell asleep. I had a nightmare of him shooting drugs with a gun instead of a syringe.

Although I obeyed his wishes, the guilt was crushing. No other incidents happened during the remaining week and a half of vacation. I thought it would lift Phil's mood to visit a butterfly museum. Like everything else, he found it boring. He seemed irritated with us, with me especially. He scratched at his torso, arms, and legs—his eyes were bloodshot. My parents must have noticed but pretended not to. And I was complicit, tired of trying to fix everything. Besides, I was doing all I could to fight off depression and the nagging feeling that my family would be better off if I died.

With every mental muscle I had, I focused on our next excursion. On Christmas day, we visited a historic cathedral. Phil thought it was dumb and asked to go to the beach instead. Dad gave in. I wondered if "beach" was code for meeting a drug dealer, and if I'd find my brother with another needle in his arm. Maybe this time he'd overdose, and it would be my fault.

My parents took me to the cathedral and its adjoining convent. A hunchback nun, who spoke English, showed us around the Spanish colonial building, leading us to the patio. A stuccoed alcove arched over an enormous Nativity scene—the figurines sculpted by nuns. The hunchbacked woman told us a sister might work a full year on a single statue. The scene featured Jesus, Mary, Joseph, the three wise men, and the hovering angel— surrounded by villagers. They reminded me of my dolls: my love for things in miniature, a world I could control. But no fantasy eased my remorse.

"Mom and Dad, Phil—"

My father interrupted, "Your brother needs rest."

I wasn't sure what Dad was referring to, but figured it would have destroyed him if he ever fully acknowledged my brother's sickness.

I gave up trying to tell my parents about the needle and vial, sure that goddamn Gun would find its way into the back of my head. Although I kept quiet, I couldn't stop the obsessive worries. Phil never joined us again, except for our last day, when we went to the rainforest, to see a *coquí*, the almost-transparent frog native to Puerto Rico. It reawakened his love of creatures. For the first time, he wasn't bored, and I saw a side of him I remembered and loved—the same person who'd doted on his pigeons.

The day we left, I introduced Phil to Rosalinda. She squawked, "¡*Hasta luego!*"

During the short flight to New York, we traveled from one reality to another. I couldn't obliterate the vision of my brother with a syringe stabbed into his arm. That stench of death wouldn't leave me. We drove back to Philadelphia—the weather colder and windier than before. I'd not only returned to the bleakness of winter, but also carried an ugly secret I couldn't tell or forget. It entered me like the drug pumping into my brother's vein. That night, in my bed at the Toot, I kept seeing his white eyes grow larger, staring into me. I gave up trying to sleep. The world outside was also white. Trees seemed to writhe under the snow's weight, searchlights intensifying the whiteness. When I turned off my lamp, those lights scoured my room's walls, their cracks like broken blood vessels in an eye.

CHAPTER 19
BURNT

Morning Meeting: Glasses listed new regulations. But I didn't give a shit. I was tired of being trapped in this place, trapped inside Phil's ugly secret. The noise in my head wouldn't stop: *He'll die, my fault.* I'd had enough. Freed by white-hot anger, I thought the unthinkable: I wished he *had* died.

I finally pricked up my ears when Glasses introduced a new patient to the ward. She asked us to applaud, as if ending up in a teen loony bin was an accomplishment. I wouldn't do it. I sat there staring at the fools who clapped because one more kid got stuck in this hellhole. Maybe I'd ignore Glasses' rules altogether. Maybe I'd no longer care about other people.

At lunch, I met the new kid: Al, short for Alton. Only adults called him that. He came from Dallas, son of a wealthy oil tycoon. Like many patients, Al couldn't "do" school. Rumors of his story made the rounds. He'd be staying in the room next to mine. Over chicken and asparagus, I talked to him, "My parents used to live in Dallas." He wasn't looking, so I talked louder, "Dad went to SMU."

"What brought 'em North?" he asked.

"A contract with the government. Dad's a lawyer."

"How long ya been in this shit hole?"

"Over a year."

He sneered.

I said, "I was in boarding school—"

"Man, the fuckin' shit parents make ya do."

"That's for sure." *Wow, this guy gets me.*

"Mine are flyin' up every month in their own plane."

"Serious?"

"My old man knows how to fly it, not much else."

"Fathers are fucking morons," I said. I liked the way it felt saying those words. Al, with his tousled hair and rock-star clothes, was the ultimate in cool. He was the kind of kid who could've gotten along with the bullies at home and at boarding school. Maybe they would've been afraid of *him.* If I became his friend, I'd make the change into a regular guy. Better yet, *I* could be a bully, and people would be afraid of me. Picking up my tray, I said, "Gotta go to O.T. You coming?"

"Fuckin' maybe, fuckin' maybe not."

He never showed up nor came around to being my friend. I was still too invested in being good. I needed to stomp out my soft feelings. They'd only made people loathe me. But when I thought I'd killed my old self, vestiges resurfaced. Being Al's friend would help me annihilate them. Then I'd do whatever I wanted and get away with it, like Phil. Archibald would even release me, out of fear.

After lunch, Cora warned me about Al. She thought he was dangerous and spoiled. Although she wasn't at liberty to say, it was obvious she couldn't stand him. I felt bad doing it, but I ignored her. She didn't understand how sick I was of being a nice boy. She looked wounded and walked away. I acted as if I didn't mind.

Next Morning Meeting: We learned Al had a history with guns and drugs. No surprise. I'd realized from the moment I met him he was like Phil. He'd be my proxy for dealing with my brother.

Al and I also had a connection: We'd both attempted suicide. Despite that, he managed to get his first excursion after one month. I'd waited eight for mine. Like Phil, he got anything he wanted. Al came back bug-eyed, wired. I seemed to be the only person to notice. The night staff looked the other way, as my parents had ignored my brother's signs. The mixture of disdain and euphoria on Al's face should have scared me, but I wouldn't let it.

His rich parents must've finagled a deal with the Toot, because he got more and more late-night outings to Center City. One night, after he came back, tapping on the wall next to my bed woke me: faster than I imagined a hand could move, continuing for hours. I was an insomniac; the sound made sleep impossible. When I pounded back, the tapping turned into thuds.

At Morning Meeting, I spoke up for the first time in the fourteen months I'd been at the Toot. "There's tapping coming from the wall next to my bed."

Al had a pleased smirk, prompting Cora to ask, "Alton, did you hear it, too?"

"Oh, fuck all of you, man! Can't you take a little creative Morse code?

Glasses snapped, "That's not—"

"Gimme a goddamn break," he said. "I couldn't sleep."

Realizing my dream of a friendship with the coolest person at the Toot could be shattered if I wasn't tactful, I said, "I get it, and it's cool, but do it on another wall."

He glared at me. After that, the tapping grew louder and lasted longer. I asked Archibald to move me to another room, but not one was available. To make up for lost sleep, I sacrificed outdoor time for naps. I also asked Cora to tell me when Al went out with his pack of "cool" kids. These were new patients who never talked to me, even though I knew some of them from Group. Al was the ringleader. They came back in the wee hours of the morning, past our curfew. Al made his own rules. I admired him for that. Nobody could see it yet, but I was becoming like him. Then, my parents, Phil, the shrinks, and even the Toot would do whatever I wanted. I had never allowed myself to feel so much anger before, and I liked it. I stayed up that night, writing instructions people would have to follow when dealing with me: *my* terms.

Although my door was shut, I heard loud arguing and cursing down the hall at two a.m. An orderly discovered Al and his stooges had come back with drugs: cocaine, methamphetamine, heroin, hashish, pot, and LSD, rolled in Saran Wrap. I wished I had been one of those kids.

At the next Morning Meeting, Glasses clutched stapled reports, as if ready to be interviewed for the news. She had the characteristics of a snitch in mob movies. She said, "We've uncovered some very dis-turbing information. Patients were caught with several thousand dollars' worth of illicit drugs last night. The intoxicants have been turned over to the police. Those caught perpetrating this crime will have rights revoked for the foreseeable future." She added that selected patients would be strip-searched after going to Center City, to prevent similar abuses. This included full-cavity probes of both sexes.

Dr. Archibald walked in late, files in hand. One of the residents whispered in his ear. Archibald's big-toothed grin dissolved. A patient of his, Al managed to get more of his concern in a short time than I had for following the rules. I felt defeated, just as I had when Phil won Dad's affections. *Fuck you, Archibald*, I thought. *You pay attention to bad kids. Wait till you see what I've got in store.* I fantasized becoming the kind of person I had always dreaded.

Glasses continued, "What we find disturbing is to think this has probably been going on for quite some time." Of course they knew. She had to say that to sound legal and sanctimonious. It was a lie.

Al looked even prouder than Glasses, a scowl carved into his elfin face. Finding the news thrillingly dangerous, I'd prove myself by becoming a friend to him and the kids involved. We knew who they were. Glasses had also found the "works"—paraphernalia for *shooting up*. I'd never heard that term before. It reminded me of The Gun.

I'd never told anyone, especially not Archibald, but I dreamed about blowing my brains out. I fixated on the verb "to shoot." I'd even written a will of sorts, demanding to have "A Day in the Life" played at my funeral. And I wanted to be cremated—no worms feasting on me.

In the Day Room, I pulled Al to the side and boasted that I'd healed my brother when he OD'd. I said I'd help Al, too, if he needed it. He sniffed. I reminded him I had a good-boy reputation to hide behind; no one would suspect me. But I wasn't that boy anymore. He sniffed again. I wasn't sure he believed me. That night, Al didn't tap on the wall.

I had a plan to become even more like Al and Phil. If I tried smoking pot, maybe I'd get close to the kids who scored dope. Chambliss smoked it regularly and said it helped her understand our readings in Matthew's classes. I wondered if she bought the weed from Al. It increased her tendency to speak of herself in third person.

She hung out with David—a Bob Dylan lookalike. An aficionado of Dylan's songs, he went over the lyrics with me. David was cool *and* nice. Concealed by the grounds' elm trees, these two friends invited me to smoke pot mixed with hashish. By some sleight of hand, they had distanced themselves from the "druggies" who were strip-searched. Chambliss and David got *their* "primo shit" from the orderlies.

"Hurts my throat," I told them, embarrassed to admit I'd never even smoked cigarettes. "And I don't feel stoned."

With a smile, David rhymed, "You'll get more sensitive to it the more you do it."

Lion Boy soon joined the three of us, and we found other hiding places, such as the laundry room and the back of the gym, where it stunk of old sneakers. We'd toke there, day after day. Eventually, the smoke no longer felt harsh but velvety—a thick carpet I floated on, beyond the stone wall.

David observed my "development," commenting on the wise things I said under the influence. I'd sometimes see daisies raining through the air and colors streaming from our mouths as we spoke—shades changing with our tones. He said the "primo shit" was cut with hashish, peyote, and other things. I never knew what. And even though it was frightening at first, I felt protected by my new friends.

On one of those days, as we traipsed across the lawn to O.T., the grass turned into fur, the flank of some gargantuan animal. The beast started breathing. Then I saw myself as a tick on its side. As in lucid dreaming, I knew it wasn't real, and yet it was no less horrifying. I couldn't wait till the sensation passed. I promised myself—no more pot, "primo" or otherwise. But I needed to be a part of this group. It was the first time in my life I had ever fit in. I couldn't let the opportunity go. These people *were* my world. I'd do *anything* to fit in. And despite their problems, they accepted and supported me more than most teens on the outside ever had.

Even though Chambliss liked me, I knew little about her. I learned she had no memory going back further than three years. I also learned she sometimes forgot who and where she was. During those times, especially, she spoke of herself in third person. Then, *bang*, she'd be back with no recollection of the blackout. Cora said the doctors weren't sure why this happened, "Nothing wrong with her brain." The shrinks thought Chambliss must have seen something so terrible her unconscious blacked it out.

Over lunch, she reminded me New Year's was coming up. She'd found an abandoned Gothic church in West Philly. She said, "The interior's stripped, leaving only the marble floor. We can make a bonfire and tell ghost stories."

I pictured flames reflecting on stained-glass windows: saints in draped robes, eyes lit from within. It seemed horribly sacrilegious.

"It'll be good luck for the New Year. Y'know, burning the past," she said.

"With a jug of Gallo, it'll be fuckin' far out. Dean, ya with us?" Lion Boy asked.

"Sure," I said, thinking wine would be less scary than pot and still might help me fit in. I had another reason: Lion Boy was friends with Al. Even though Al wasn't joining us, he'd hear I'd gone and think I was cool.

We all managed to get passes, convincing our shrinks we were going to a New Year's Eve party at the Philadelphia Museum of Art. The staff didn't even check. We strolled out the gate and continued toward the bus we would have taken to the museum. Out of view, we looped back to West Philly, approaching the church Chambliss had described. Perched on a hill, it reminded me of the Bates House. Its sign read: *The Church of the Holy. . . .*The second half was covered by graffiti and vines. We pried open a broken door. Inside, it smelled of wet dust and piss. A rat scampered by. We gathered pieces of furniture to use as kindling—a chair leg, a drawer, and rectangular slabs of plywood, strewn as if someone had started to repair the church but abandoned it. We piled the pieces in the middle of the marble floor, so the flames wouldn't burn the walls. Lion Boy scrunched newspaper between the kindling. Chambliss lit the matches. The fire caught slowly, jaggedly, then raged. Seated across from me, my friends' faces looked disembodied above the flames. We drank and sang. Drank and told stories. Drank and laughed, the room tilting and spinning.

"My grandmother would call this blasphemy," I said as a piece of kindling snapped, sparks sizzling into the rafters.

"Not at all—we're communing like the ancients," Chambliss said.

"*With* the ancients!" David corrected. "Look—the Tree of Life!"

We craned our necks, our eyes scanning the flames. But no tree.

"What's it doing?" Chambliss said.

David closed his eyes. "Cords strung from branches like a harp."

"Why?" I asked.

"The spirits are playing."

"Playing what?" I said. He didn't answer.

Lion Boy peeled off his shirt. Although I was getting sick, I noticed his pectorals, softly dusted with light brown hair, tapering into the waist of his jeans. He had the smallest nipples I'd ever seen, and in the swirling light, tiny blond hairs lit up against his sweaty skin. Trickles of perspiration followed the contours of his body. Without anyone noticing, I slid next to him, wanting to breathe his scent.

Chambliss managed to stay sober. "We ought to go to the Dunkin' Donuts and get you boys some black coffee."

"No way," Lion Boy said. "We're flyin'."

David rocked his head back and forth. "Can you hear?"

"Let's do a séance!" Lion Boy extended his arms.

"Great Spirit, I hear your voice in the winds—hear *me*!" David's head fell limp.

I wanted to run but suppressed the urge.

"Well, boys, the spirits won't communicate with us much longer—we're out of kindling. Wine's gone, too." Chambliss stood up, empty jug in hand.

We waited a few minutes for David to come out of his trance. He looked weak, so he leaned on me. Not stopping to see if the flames had died out, we stumbled down the block. For all we knew, we could have set the church on fire.

Once we got to Dunkin' Donuts, Chambliss ordered coffee and donuts for us. But the sight of the gooey desserts sent Lion Boy and me bolting to the bathroom, puking.

Footsteps. The bathroom door opened. "You boys okay?" a policeman asked.

"Yeah, sure, Officer," I managed to say. His presence sobered us up more than the Styrofoam cups of coffee. With Chambliss as our guide, we made our way back to the Toot, quietly entered the ward, trying not to look drunk. I went straight to bed, having to get up early the next morning: visiting day. I was proud of myself, having stripped away another layer of good-boy Dean. And I finally had friends.

I woke with a punishing hangover. I couldn't conceive of ever getting drunk again. The walls seemed to flutter like sheets of tin, and bells kept clanging in my ears. I thought they'd never stop. I took a long shower, the water soothing my head. Toweling off, I looked out the window and noticed Mom and Dad had arrived in a new car. I tugged on clothes and sneakers, meeting them by the nurse's station for a day pass.

"The head nurse told us you missed Morning Meeting," Dad said.

"Couldn't get up."

"Why's that?"

"Got sick."

"You mean drunk?"

"Um ..."

"You don't think they keep us informed of your behavior?" he asked. Mom was silent. I hoped she'd pipe in on my behalf.

I had been bad for once in my life, and people liked me. "Sorry, I guess."

"You *guess*?"

"It was supposed to, ya know. . . ."

"Supposed to *what*?"

"Throw old inhibitions aside."

We climbed into the new car and drove to Bucks County. I had always been honest with my parents, thanks to the pact Mom made with me as a kid: If I told the truth, they wouldn't spank me. Instead, we'd find a solution for what I'd done wrong. This came after years of Dad's whipping us with his belt (once hitting me in the eye) and Mom spanking us with her hairbrush (after which she wept). The new policy sprang from her reading Dr. Benjamin Spock, who encouraged children's honesty. Punishments—he reasoned—prevented it. The technique worked. Truth was, feeling guilty over my misconduct had always been more painful than any punishment. That's why swallowing the secret about Phil's syringe was unbearable; it destroyed that bond. The remorse had gnawed at me, but I'd finally put an end to it.

Going along with the bonfire and drinking, I'd crossed a boundary. Determined to recast myself as someone popular, I saw it working. I'd spent so much of my childhood locked up in my bedroom, doing homework till it was perfect, getting straight A's in everything but math. But perfect was never good enough.

Before I was shipped off to boarding school, Phil began his descent into booze and drugs. Policemen carried him home, finding him at the mall—bloody and incoherent. As Mayor and Public Safety Director, Dad had the authorities expunge his records. Somehow, I believed I'd achieved good grades at my brother's expense. I didn't deserve *them* or happiness. Getting drunk was the first step in reversing my image, even if it involved dishonesty. My newfound anger made me invincible. After we had an awkward lunch in Doylestown, Dad drove us back to the Toot.

Mom cleared her throat, saying she had something to announce: They were getting divorced the following week. They'd separated so many times I never knew their current status. The new car was hers. Was she asking me to condone the divorce? Their blighted marriage had been the main reason they and Dr. Sachs had sent me to Bakely.

Divorce would be the easy part. Why had no one protected me from their endless screaming and that stupid Gun? They were breaking free of each other, but *I* was locked up. I was pissed off but wouldn't show it. "You'll still be my parents?" I asked.

"Of course, we'd never stop loving you," Mom said.

"She's right, Son," Dad added.

"Will you call me when it's done?" I imagined I'd *feel* when it happened before she called, the way some people know when a loved one dies. Mom nodded.

To the side of the road, I spotted a dead deer, its neck broken. Its eyes glistened, reflecting the car lights. Those sad, dead eyes seemed to mirror my emotions.

Our headlights tunneled a path in the road lined with sugar maples, leading to the Toot. I hugged my parents, mouthed, *I love you*, and drifted inside without waving good-bye. I felt like I'd stepped out of my body.

Chapter 20
Cabal

An obsession with death shadowed me. News of my parents' approaching divorce triggered the fixation. I felt disconnected from my family and my body.

Meanwhile, Matthew was teaching us about ancient Egypt, a death-obsessed culture. He took us to the University of Pennsylvania Museum, to explore the Egyptians' lapis-lazuli world. We came upon the mummies and stood there, staring. The tour guide explained how the embalmer-priest had slashed open the corpse with a copper scalpel. The one in the case was oxidized a deep blue-green. The embalmer then snaked a hook up the nose, dragging out brain morsels, like a plumber clearing a pipe. The priest removed organs, purified the body, and wound the corpse with linen— preparing it for eternity. I pictured the slicing to be precise, antiseptic, surgical. Dying in this culture seemed elevated to an art. The ritualistic aspect reminded me of how I'd buried my dolls.

Back at the Toot, I thought about the word *wound*— the past tense of *wind* or a deep gash. That brought back the image of Terri's glistening blood. Shortly thereafter, I had asked her why she did it. I thought she wanted to die, but she said it was a way of making bad feelings dissolve. She had to be controlled, she said, avoiding veins and arteries. Afraid of infections, she flushed the metal nail file with scalding water. Little did she know, but she was giving me instructions.

Hoping sunshine and cold air would scour away my suicidal thoughts, I wandered the grounds, spotting a broken Coke bottle. It glinted, tempting me to pluck it from the lawn. Its color reminded me of that ancient scalpel. Making sure no one was looking, I pocketed the fragment and headed back to my room. I thought of myself as an embalmer-priest. I washed the shard in hot water, to make sure I didn't get an infection. The cutting had to be clean and artful, avoiding veins and arteries.

The way I used to dig up my dolls to see what death looked like, I wanted to understand my body's red river. I positioned the fragment above my left arm—fought off the fear of hurt, pushing beyond limitations. I pressed the sharp edge to my delicate underarm. The shard felt smooth and warm. Then, I sawed in timid swipes— deeper, back and forth, more forcefully. I felt my body pulsing, vibrant. I was no longer disconnected from it. As I watched my blood course, I respected the workings of my nervous system. I crossed boundaries, from frightening pang to delicious pain to sheer elation.

It seemed like the first time I'd felt *anything*. It blocked out excruciating thoughts. The warmth I'd felt, after taking the noose from my neck, filled my head again. Everything blossomed. As the hacking revealed pinker layers of skin, then gushing red, I knew I was different. What would horrify most people thrilled me.

It was also punishment for my parents' divorce, for my brother's shooting up, for my being in this place. If I died, all would be forgiven. I welcomed death. There'd be a eulogy. My family would cry and say how much they loved and missed me, but it would be too late, for them at least. I'd be *free*. I loved that word, polishing it in my mouth, saying it over and over. Maybe I'd never get free of the Toot. Maybe *this* was the way out.

Even so, I was conflicted. I didn't want to die just *yet*. I had a technique for lessening depression. And I had friends, real friends. Most of them were girls, "cutters," so we'd be closer. They'd understand me, even if the stupid adults didn't.

I watched my arm's blood spiral like a liquid rose, dissolving into the sink. Retreating to that blank place where neither thoughts nor words can reach, I became quiet. I wound my arm with toilet paper, sealed the bandage with Scotch tape, slid on a long-sleeved shirt. Strolling back to the dining room, I felt more peaceful than before—floating. I'd achieved a new experience, an accomplishment. No adult could find out. If they did, I'd get locked in I.C.U., losing excursion privileges. I knew the rules. I didn't even tell my cutter friends, though I was aching to. Even Chambliss, I'd recently learned, had a history of it, which is why she always wore long sleeves.

The following day at O.T., I complained about not having graphite pencils that varied in softness. Opening a drawer, the therapist showed me a selection: 6B to 2H.

"Great, do you have blades too?" I asked, adding that artists aren't supposed to use a pencil sharpener, but a razor blade and sandpaper.

"Yeah, but you comprehend the policy," said the therapist. "Here's the box; use one and give it back, pronto."

I took out two when no one was looking. Both were covered in little cardboard folders. I slipped one into my pocket. Opening the other, I sharpened three pencils, tucked the razor blade in the box and handed it back to the therapist. "Here—thanks." I put the used one on top, scared she'd count the number of blades in the box. But she didn't. I'd earned everyone's trust.

That night, after dinner, I felt the pull to do it again. The aroma of broiled chicken and slightly burnt butter drifted down the hall. My room had its own scents: the dusty smell of electric heat and freshly changed linens. I closed my door and went into the bathroom. Its harsh light and tiled surfaces focused my thoughts. I tugged the blade from my pocket, peeled its folder, ran it over my thumb. Sharp enough. I stretched my left arm across the porcelain sink. There was nothing to be afraid of: I was facing something sacred. Gentle sawing. Less irritating with a sharp razor blade. My skin reddened, blood sluicing to the surface. No stopping. Deeper. Blood swirled from my arm. So much of it, I couldn't see the wound. The sink was marbleized with bloody water. Peace filled my head with spinning lights, as if I were surrounded by an enormous kaleidoscope. I was both thrillingly alive *in* my body and freed *from* it, as if I had died.

But there was no hiding this laceration with toilet paper and a long-sleeved shirt. The wound streamed. Not intending to carve my arm so deeply, I was mad at myself for not being more precise. I had the presence of mind to hide the razor blade, then wrapped a towel around my arm, and marched stoically to the nurse's station. In the time it took to get there, the white terrycloth had turned bright red. I had never seen so much blood gushing from my body. The cloth couldn't contain it. A trail of blood drops followed me like red tears. I banged on the glass of the nurse's station. A bleach-blond nurse saw me. She ran out, jawing, *Oh, God*. Tightening the towel into a tourniquet, she told me to hold it, and hurried me upstairs to the clinic. The gash required six stitches, which hurt more than the razor blade. But ecstasy floated through me, like the saints' mortification of the flesh my grandmother had told me about. Neither nurses nor doctors understood: I was in control. The blond nurse walked me to I.C.U., where I spent the night: an achievement. I wasn't invisible anymore.

The following morning, Cora escorted me back to the ward, looking disappointed. I wished I could have explained it to her, but we didn't share a word. We arrived at the ward early enough to hear the conversation turn to me at Morning Meeting.

"We were all rather upset to learn Dean wounded himself so badly he required stitches. To my understanding, it's the first time he's done this. Dean, is that right?" Glasses asked.

"The first one *you* know about."

"I'm sure Dr. Archibald will be addressing this issue on an individual basis. Is there anything going on that made you do it?"

"Sick of it."

"Sick of what?"

"This prison."

"Surely, this kind of behavior isn't going to get you released."

My eyes fixed on the synthetic carpet's cigarette burns.

"Your privileges are withheld, *again*. We can't have you doing yourself in—not on my shift," she said, making sure everyone heard.

Terri ran over to me, threw her arms around my shoulders, and said, "Ignore that ice-bitch, baby. We love you. Don't be doin' crazy shit like the rest of us."

"Terri, your outburst will have to be articulated some other time," Glasses said, rifling through papers.

Terri said, "Look what this fuckin' place does to people, what *you* do to people. So high-and-mighty. The whole time, you just want the guys around here to fuck you!"

Glasses started to answer Terri, "You're perilously close—"

But Terri interrupted her, "On a goddamn ego trip, takin' us all down. You fuckin'. . . ." Terri bolted from Morning Meeting, as she had from countless Group sessions, crying toward her room.

I had spent years protecting other people. When I needed someone to take my side, I was usually on my own. My vision blurred. Chambliss, David, Lion Boy, and other kids circled me in a mass embrace. I couldn't believe what was happening. I thanked them and said I was okay, thinking they'd go on about their activities. Instead, they stayed. I assured them I was fine, to give them the excuse to forget about me. But something was different. They understood me in a way that no one else had—even more than I could. I was embarrassed to receive so much affection. But as I had broken through fear in the act of cutting, I broke another boundary: I let them care about me. They said I was one of them;

they'd be there for me. I allowed them to crack through the shell I'd built to protect myself from bullies. I pressed my head to my chest, tears running, not caring if anyone saw. Their embrace radiated throughout the room.

I was loved.

I loved.

"There'll be volleyball practice in half an hour," Glasses announced. "Morning Meeting's over."

I hugged my friends, saying I wished I knew a word bigger than "Thanks," so I could give it to them like a gift. After we untangled our arms and tear-wet sleeves, Chambliss handed me a tissue. I noticed the scars on her arm.

"You guys are amazing, but I'm worried about Terri." I shuffled to her room—its door ajar. "Terri, thanks for speaking up for me. No one ever—"

"Sweetie, don't you see, you don't belong in this place."

"At least I have friends here."

"And we're all swimmin' together in this fuckin' virus soup. It ain't helpin' nobody."

"Good luck getting shrinks to believe that."

"Dean, you ever done this before?"

"Not before I came here, but I tried hanging myself. And I have a fantasy."

"What kind?"

"About a gun."

"*What?*"

"I picture shooting myself in the head."

"Your fuckin' brains would be all over the room!"

"But the fantasy makes the scary feelings go away."

"Don't ever do that as long as I'm here. Promise?"

"Okay, for your sake." I grabbed her hand, not saying another word. Unable to talk or move, we held each other for at least an hour.

Though I vowed never to shoot myself, it wasn't hard to be pushed to slash again. A short list of prompts: happy kids on TV, Group Therapy, Glasses' snide comments, Archibald's sexual questions, Peggy yelled at by a nurse, a violent patient straitjacketed.

After another "incident," orderlies ransacked my room, confiscating the blade. Big deal—I'd be inventive. One day after lunch, I took a plastic knife back to my bathroom. Even though the slow sawing hurt more, I was stoic. I made the slit superficial so I wouldn't need stitches and could cover it with a shirt. No one found out. However, that whirling, full-of-light feeling had vanished. It was just a plastic knife cutting into meat, *my* meat. It struck me as disgusting. And at a time when I was enjoying my O.T. projects, this activity left me increasingly empty.

But I was determined to get back that high. Two weeks later, I used another shard, found on the lawn, sharper than the first one. This time, I went deeper than anticipated, getting stitches again. Archibald revoked my privileges. While I loved being part of a blood cabal, the act didn't calm me for long. The fleeting relief left me with shame, like a drunken man who sobers up, only to realize he's done something awful. Concerned I'd cut again, staff looked in on me throughout the day.

When Mandrill showed up in my room, I said my left arm was already a mess, and I was fighting the urge to slash my thighs. I wanted to get that euphoric feeling back but doubted I could. He said other patients had similar sensations and those had also diminished. He thought that was a good sign.

Instead of answering, I stole a glimpse of myself in the mirror. I hated my looks, ugly and deformed, as if my emotions had manifested on my face. And I had another humiliation: I'd have to hide the marks forever. In my vulnerable state, I asked for help.

He told me if I wanted to stop cutting, I'd have to admit I was addicted to it. I saw no way to break the craving. He reminded me I was already fifteen. In only three years, I'd no longer be a minor. After all this madness was over, I'd be an adult on a beach in a bathing suit, trying to look sexy and would regret the disfigurements. I envisioned having mutilated my whole body, a mass of scar tissue— looking like a monster, more hideous than I already felt. That thought was intolerable. By talking about a future, he unlocked me from my present.

But I knew I could only move forward if I were honest. I had to come clean about having stolen the razor blade. I divulged my secret to the art therapist and apologized. Instead of being angry, she asked if I'd replace my compulsion for slicing with my love of painting. She had gotten new gouache paints and wanted to teach me how to make collagraphs—collages coated with gesso and inked like woodblocks—one of the few printing methods not to require sharp tools. She showed me examples other patients had done. I'd never seen such mysterious, hazy textures. I couldn't wait to make one. She said she'd stay later so I could spend more time at O.T. We made a pact that every time I wanted to hurt myself, I'd funnel those feelings into art, no matter how ugly or disturbing the images. I committed them to paper, where eventually they stayed.

CHAPTER 21
FIGURES IN THE SNOW

I overheard Lion Boy, Al, and other patients talking about "acid," or LSD. They claimed the new formula was stronger than before. Before what, I had no idea. But I moved toward them, making it clear I wanted to join their conversation.

"We're goin' to the Electric Factory for a concert," Al said, looking at me.

Flushed at having gotten his attention, I felt like I'd made it. Keeping up my nonchalant exterior, I asked, "Who's playing?"

"What the fuck does it matter? We're droppin' acid before we go, Cozy Toes. If you can be cool, you can come," he said. "Cozy Toes" was his attempt to be clever with my last name. Wondering why he never answered my question, I was, nonetheless, thrilled to be included— invited by him to a concert. All my efforts to fit in were paying off.

"Sure," I said, pushing aside my earlier promise to avoid drugs. In agreeing to drop acid, I was tearing off another layer of resistance, flaying my good-boy self alive. I'd heard stories of people who became catatonic after just one acid trip and others who had flashbacks for years. I was scared as hell, but I had become a bully toward the gentler part of myself. When fears surfaced, I shoved them down with a defiant "no." I was proud of how unfeeling I'd become. Al's interest in being my friend was proof that I'd beaten myself into shape. Besides, rock musicians I admired admitted to having dropped acid. They said it made them more creative; that's what it would do for me.

The following day, after dinner, Al, Chambliss, Lion Boy, Terri, David, a new girl, and I met on the darkened lawn. Chambliss doled out the blotter acid—a priestess with her devotees. Her bell-shaped sleeves made the process seem sacred. "Let it stay on your tongue like a Communion wafer," she told us.

I convinced myself this would be a less gruesome way to recapture the ecstasy I'd experienced after gashing my arm, when a wave of release—from all the sadness and rage—made me feel shimmeringly alive.

After dropping the acid, we all headed toward the parking lot, to meet our chaperone, Matthew. The Toot asked him to join us to prevent further drug abuse on the outside, never acknowledging it was rampant on the ward—a virtual drug supermarket.

At the concert, where several rock bands played, I kept expecting to see huge spirals and brightly colored flowers throbbing to the music. Halfway through the event, the new girl reacted badly to the acid and darted downstairs, holding her head, saying it was going to explode. Chambliss and I rushed to comfort her. We told Matthew the girl was suffering from a migraine.

Although I saw nothing strange during the concert, as we drove back, snow fell in violet swirls, intricate and precise. When I stepped from the car, the snow took on paisley patterns, wriggling into amoebas. Matthew drove away, but we stayed on the lawn in the dark, perched on icy Adirondack chairs.

Chambliss slipped off her beaded bracelet. "Look, it's a snake!" she said.

Terrified it was poisonous, I lied, "Gotta go to bed. This is making me tired." There was too much commotion in my head for me to sleep. Back in my room, I looked out the window and was shocked to see a flood of light break open from the sky—night became day. In that beam, I saw Marilyn Monroe in a red dress. She was fencing with a dark, swirling mass like the Death Fist I'd fought off in a dream after my suicide attempt. Marilyn leaped and jabbed. When I looked away, she unexpectedly appeared on the arm of my easy chair. She sobbed, face in hands. I blinked and made her disappear. I blinked and made her reappear.

Overwhelmed, I lay down, but instead of sleeping, I floated up out of my body, which writhed below me on the bed: a piece of raw, bloody meat. Shocked by the disgusting image, I was yanked back into my body. Volts of electricity shot through my arms. I couldn't move or think. Forearms locked, fists clenched, I stared at my pillow. It glowed with the most brilliant red I had ever seen. I *heard* the color hammering in my eardrums. Synaesthesia returned, multiplied a hundred times. Black ciphers—part hieroglyph, part rune, part alchemical symbol—flickered onto my pillowcase. One cluster of symbols lasted a minute, replaced by another and another. I knew this was some important message meant only for me and tried frantically to decode it but couldn't.

My temples pulsated. I stayed awake the whole night. By about six in the morning, I finally closed my eyes, only to be awakened for breakfast an hour later. Walking from my room, I felt like Dorothy emerging from her fallen house, in reverse: Everything was black-and-white. I kept shaking my head and rubbing my eyes, thinking I could coax color back. Dazed, I wandered the halls: Everything looked like an old movie. I was petrified. Maybe I'd altered my brain and eyes, unable to enjoy art. My worst fear: I'd never paint again. Stupid me—trading color for acceptance. This was retribution. I wanted desperately to go for help, to tell a nurse, to tell Archibald, but I didn't trust them—aware that I'd lose my privileges. And I'd have to snitch on Al.

Cora sensed something was wrong. I said I was coming down with the flu. When I told Chambliss my head was still galloping and buzzing all at once, she revealed the acid had been "cut" with speed. She asked me to wait and disappeared into her room to rummage through a stash of pills. She returned with some Thorazine tablets, which she instructed me to take. She said it was the antidote to LSD. It would quiet my mind, stop the hallucinations, and allow me to sleep. I had to turn these horrible delusions off. I was scared I'd go insane otherwise, and I desperately needed sleep. More to the point, I trusted her over the nurses and doctors. I finally woke hours later, right before dinner. I told Al what I'd done, to impress him.

"So fuckin' what? You don't even remember the concert." The more he rejected me, the more his approval mattered. He told me he was going on another excursion to hear a new band but didn't mention their name. I asked if I could come. To my surprise, he said I could if kept my mouth shut. His warnings sounded like Phil's.

I had to get the outing cleared with a shrink. Mandrill, like a lenient parent, was lax about these things. Or maybe he didn't care. He acted as if the Toot and everyone in it were a joke. So much the better. I got my Friday-night pass to see The Castle Crows, a group whose name I'd made up. Mandrill didn't check to see if such a group even existed. My ability to play this system had become crafty.

Al didn't want to be seen walking out with me—said it would look suspicious. I thought he'd be embarrassed. Nonetheless, I stuck to our plan. After dinner, I left the ward, crossed the lawn to the Old Building, where I watched till he slunk past the wall. I waited five minutes before following him. We met in front of a vacant topless bar four blocks away, its broken windows replaced by plywood covered in graffiti. Color had returned to my vision after a week. Dayglow pink-and-chartreuse tags read: *Lover Boy, King o' the World, Killa.* We took the subway and switched for a bus. We rode without speaking for at least half an hour, entering bleaker and bleaker parts of North Philadelphia. Abandoned buildings. Doors nailed shut with boards. Men huddled secretively in alcoves, indistinct from their shadows. Other people lay on sidewalks, clutching plastic bags. Liquid leaked from their crotches as if their bodies wept, leaving dark trails on the sidewalk. I'd heard that when a person dies, the body releases its fluids. I thought these were corpses and wondered if I'd end up like them. But nothing deterred me. I was getting Al's approval.

We came to an abandoned house—gangs' tags and symbols spray-painted all over it: a bleeding sun, a pistol, a tombstone. I followed Al up the creaking stairs. Second floor. Third floor. The hallways reeked of bug spray. He knocked on a door. A man with glassy, vacant eyes opened it, said nothing. I worried about standing out in my purple top hat, which I'd worn thinking we were going to a rock concert.

People slumped in chairs throughout the room, many with eyes shut or flickering. I heard vomiting and choking from the back. It smelled like I'd returned to that hotel room in Puerto Rico, or entered a recurring nightmare I had of rotting people. I wanted to bolt but forced myself not to *be* myself.

"Into snow?" Al asked.

"Whadya mean?"

"Y'know—horse, smack. The opposite of acid—no weird shit. In fact, you won't give a damn about nothin'. If ya ever had a conscience, kiss it goodbye. "

"Oh," I said. This seemed a lot less scary than acid. Maybe this is what Phil had injected in that hotel. I could stop feeling responsible for him. The bonus was I got to earn Al's approval. I'd happily sacrifice myself to be free of myself.

I couldn't say no. Al told me to tie a rubber tube around my left arm and pump it up to get "a nice fat vein." Disconnected from my body, I'd become an automaton, obeying his orders.

"My friend's cookin' the stuff," he said.

I imagined Al protecting me, falling in love with me. He took money from his wallet, paid my share. I thought, *I've made it.*

"Oh yeah, look at that big fuckin' juicy one," he said, piercing my vein:

White,

white,

white ...

Everything went blank and full of a light I had never seen before ... I collapsed into a ratty chair. Floated miles away. Flew with wings made of snow, wings pushing through clouds. Saw my body and the world, luminous. I smiled at Al and his friends, miles from fear, remorse, and any conscience. Had someone killed my beloved grandmother right before my eyes, I would have smiled.

"He's a natural. Fuckin' loves this shit," one of the goons said. "He'll be back."

On the way out, Al fastidiously weighed, cut, and wrapped packets of the white powder in tin foil and Saran Wrap. "Here, you're carryin' these. Got it?" he said.

"Okay," I answered.

"No one's gonna check innocent Cozy Toes, or you ain't comin' back for more.

"As long as I don't have to stick them up my butt."

"What the fuck you talkin' about? Ya got coat pockets, right?"

"Sure."

"That's the good thing about comin' here with you. They won't search *you* for drugs."

"But they might for blades."

"Get that the fuck outta your head. It's gonna make you paranoid, then you *will* get checked."

I figured out what my role had been. But I was using Al, too. I was exterminating myself. Al and I went back to the smack den one more time. Then we brought twice the amount of "junk" and works to the Toot. I carried it all, still unsuspected. I even learned how to use the syringe.

One night, I decided to do it on my own. I cooked the mixture in my bathroom with a spoon, sat on the toilet, a necktie around my left arm, slid the needle's bevel into my vein, shoved the plunger in. I staggered to my bedroom, collapsed onto my bed. I lay there for what must have been an hour and a half. Finally, able to walk again, I put on my top hat. In a trance, I got a pass and floated out the front door. I felt nothing.

Through the glass hallway, to the Old Building—I spotted Peggy. Knowing her since childhood, I felt comforted by her, as though she were family. She sat in an antique chair below portraits of former trustees, singing, "People from before swim in yesterday never dusty they didn't know they were from a book Mommy used to read."

The rhythm of her voice and childlike words carried me away. We sat together for the next hour: me in shoulder-length hair and purple top hat, she in a housedress and lopsided wig. The portraits loomed above us, cracks in the darkened paint seeming to breathe. I was grateful Peggy didn't expect me to answer. I couldn't talk, didn't want to; words would stain this perfect blankness. Feeling that nothing could harm me ever again, I dozed off, finally nudged awake by a nurse. In the meantime, Peggy had vanished. The nurse escorted me back to the ward, writing up the "episode." I apologized, claiming my insomnia had been especially bad.

The following day, I managed to wake early enough for breakfast. While I sat slurping oatmeal, Cora rushed over to my table to tell me I had a phone call in the conference room.

Mom whispered over the phone, "It's done." I could tell from the tightness of her voice she was holding back tears. It was that simple: She and Dad were divorced. It had come after their one-month separation. Their on-again-off-again relationship was its very nature. I doubted they'd ever have the nerve to really end it. But like that—it was over. I wondered where Dad and Phil were, and how they were reacting. I didn't ask and risk upsetting Mom.

Here was the day I'd dreaded most of my life. I expected to hear something like a dynamite blast. Instead, all four of us drifted into silence. I thanked her for letting me know and said it was for the best. I still felt the residual effect of the drug deadening my emotions. As snow covers a city, transforming cars, trash cans, and fire escapes into an enchanted world, heroin transformed my grief into apathy.

When I hung up, I didn't speak. The way I'd lost the ability to see colors for eight days, I became aloof the following week, speaking only when spoken to and only in monosyllables. It was like feeling in black-and-white.

Chapter 22
The Staircase

Applause: Another new patient arrived on the unit. Unwilling to celebrate her fate, I looked down until the clapping ended. The girl looked embarrassed by all the attention. Still taciturn after my parents' divorce, I wasn't in the mood to talk to her. But I was curious.

Realizing that Cora spoke to nurses about patients, I asked about the fifteen-year-old girl, Lenore. It violated protocol, but Cora sometimes told me what she'd learned. She wasn't a gossip; she thought we could support each other better if we understood one another's problems. She possessed a depth of compassion I rarely saw in nurses and psychiatrists. I learned that before coming to the Toot, Lenore had stayed at a "physical hospital." She had slashed her arm so deeply, she needed sixty stitches. She was a schizophrenic, Cora said, asking if I knew what that meant. I said I had a vague idea. She explained how people with that condition had a distorted view of reality. What everyone else might see as a glass of water could appear to be a glass of blood. I imagined it would be like tripping on LSD all the time—that made me shudder.

I had seen the same dazed expression on other patients and wondered if Lenore was on Thorazine, a medication given to schizophrenics (the one I'd taken to come down from acid). The new girl also reminded me of faces in Victorian engravings—large, gray eyes and rippling hair.

"What can I do for her, Cora?" I asked.

"She hears bad voices. Pray for her."

"Maybe I can be her friend."

At O.T., Lenore drew pictures of women with long hair swirling like pastel tornadoes. They had faces at first, but she erased them. That's how she "finished" her drawings. Having never seen artwork like hers, I was mesmerized. "Their hair's important," I said.

Lenore kept sketching.

"This one's got lavender hair—that one's green. Amazing colors," I added.

She turned to me, smiled, and said, "Like a garden."

That was answer enough. I understood her need to create without explanations. This was the kind of companion I'd longed for—someone who could understand me, a friendship like the one I'd had with Katie.

Lenore's aura was magical. We communicated without speaking. In our silence, we understood each other more and more, realizing how little the boxes of words contain. She was even someone I didn't have to change myself for. She liked me exactly as I was.

Heading to the other counter, where I could still see her, I found a set of gouache tubes I'd hidden in a drawer so no one else could use them. I felt a bit guilty depriving other patients of these expensive English paints. But not that guilty. *How wonderful*, I thought, *a friend who loves to draw and paint.* I offered the set to Lenore. Her face lit up when she saw it: Winsor & Newton Designers Gouache Colour Paint Set. We both loved the British spelling of *colour.* We agreed that it *looked* like the essence of color. We felt the same way about *grey*, as opposed to *gray*. She said those British spellings tasted better when she spoke them. I said I also enjoyed the way certain words felt on my mouth, like *innumerable*. We repeated that word, laughing in agreement. I then tried my synaesthesia game on her, calling out a number and asking what color she associated with it. The dull, vacant look in her eyes quickly disappeared, replaced with attentiveness. Despite the antipsychotic medications she took, her mind was agile. Few people saw that side of her. Increasingly thrilled to work with her, I looked forward to O.T. even more than before. Over the next weeks, we spent afternoons there together, lost in our art world. Aside from Matthew's classes, nothing made me happier. Lenore and I looked at and talked about each other's drawings. Whatever she said about my work was just what I needed to hear. Having met her made me think that I *had* been smart in getting committed to the Toot. We would never have met otherwise.

Eventually, I invited her to the Old Building to read poems in the marble lounge below the gallery of portraits. We thought the word *Poe-try* was named after Poe. Her favorite poem was "The Raven." It swirled obsessively around her name. In those hours, the Toot vanished. Our wounded relationship with the world mended. We thought of ourselves as a kind of cult, as if what we did made us special. We included Chambliss and David, who became as fond of Lenore as I was. Terri liked her, too, but with reservations. She wouldn't say more, seeing how much Lenore's friendship meant to me.

As weeks passed, without her cutting, I started thinking all the shrinks were wrong about her. Maybe she had gone beyond those episodes and no longer needed to hurt herself. I, too, had gone weeks without an incident and was sure to get excursion privileges. And did I ever want them—a van Gogh exhibition was coming to the Philadelphia Museum of Art, the largest ever mounted in the States. We had been studying his life and paintings in class. Matthew discussed how the painter had worked as a minister going into mines to comfort the miners, like Christ descending into Hades. Turning his back on his uncle's European gallery chain, Vincent had to live off his brother. Then the move to Arles, where the painter's mental health got worse. Even though everybody fixated on his cutting off his ear (not the whole ear, we learned), the fact that grabbed me involved a gun. There it was—the thing I'd lived in fear of as a boy, the thing I'd fantasized about using on myself. Van Gogh shot himself with a pistol after finishing a landscape of a wheat field peppered with crows. They seemed to have exploded from his heart upon the bullet's impact. A twisting path lurched to an abrupt halt in the middle of the field.

"Look at the intuitive brushstrokes in the later paintings," Matthew said, holding up an art book. Each meticulous dab seemed to move on its own. "Was he a misfit or a mystic?"

I smiled, encouraged that being a misfit might make you a better artist, despite the toll it took—or because of it. That caught Lenore's attention, too. She looked up. All the more reason we had to see the exhibit. Luckily, our doctors approved the outing. Her shrink, not affiliated with the Toot and seldom there, was even more lenient than Mandrill. They had us promise we'd look out for each other. We signed the ledger at the nurse's station, took our laminated passes, walked out the unlocked door.

It was early February, the wind bitingly cold. We darted across the lawn in a shortcut to the exit. Lenore's hair floated like the hair-tornadoes of her drawings. Outside, a left, another left. We passed West Jesuit, a respected boys' academy where we heard a brass band playing "The Stripper." That it came from a Catholic school made us laugh almost all the way to the bus stop (the same one where I had waited with Al). Lenore started doing a slinky walk in sync with the striptease music. Seeing her, of all people, do this made me laugh even harder. Snot ran from my nose—I couldn't catch my breath.

Lenore handed me a tissue and said, "Think about Glasses. That'll make you stop." Sure enough, the antidote worked.

Along the way, I helped Lenore peel circus posters from telephone poles, so she could bring them back to her room. She had been gluing a collage made of red-and-yellow clown posters to one of her walls. She needed more faces to finish it.

The bus finally came—we climbed inside. Facing a row of passengers, I worried they all knew we were kids from a loony bin. But a more shocking fear eclipsed that one: I couldn't make out the boundaries between me and other people. It was as if an invisible dividing line I'd always taken for granted had suddenly vanished. My body no longer contained me, like the night I floated above its raw meat. This bizarre awareness spooked the hell out of me. I couldn't stop it, assuming it was a residual effect of the LSD. Ever since being branded with crazy-germs, I had been judged against that label. I stifled this scary, new perception, without telling Lenore. I needed to be stable for her.

I resisted seeing her as the label, "schizophrenic." It seemed as cruel as crazy-germs. Apart from sharing our love of art and poetry, I knew little about her personal life. I hadn't wanted to pry, so I didn't ask. But on the bus, she revealed she came from a poor family, who couldn't afford the Toot for long. The alternative: a state institution. I'd heard they were violent, dismal places, little better than prisons. Maybe worse. I wouldn't let myself think about her future: I didn't want to be robbed of her friendship or imagine someone so gentle subjected to a brutal fate. There had to be a better solution. I'd ask Dad what legal options she might have. I thought for sure he would know.

We finally got there. The Philadelphia Museum of Art loomed in the distance, behind a fountain and a sea of marble stairs. People in Philly called the museum the "Greek Garage," but I found it awe-inspiring.

Lenore would point to things that caught her eye. A gesture of her hand made me see details I would've otherwise ignored, such as the pleating shadows of our legs as we climbed the steps. We made our way through hordes of museumgoers. I told her I'd been going there since I was a boy. "Ever been here before?" I asked.

"No, I'm from Cleveland."

"I'll show you my favorite places."

"Like?"

"Like walking through a magic door into different countries."

Her face broadened into a smile.

"Then there's the Marcel Duchamp collection," I said.

"The what?"

"Remember when Matthew taught us about that funny art movement—Dada? Duchamp was like the president of it."

"Did he ever start one called Mama?"

"Don't get me laughing again," I said.

"Let's see his paintings."

"Sure, there's other stuff, too."

"Sculpture?"

"Sort of."

"What's a sort-of sculpture?"

"A bird cage full of fake ice cubes and an upside-down urinal."

Lenore started laughing, which I thought was a good sign.

"The most famous thing," I said, "is a painting called *Nude Descending a Staircase*." We clattered down another corridor, entered a room, and found ourselves in front of it: Its colors shifted in a continuous thrum. The figure lunged forward from a piston at its pelvis. While descending, the nude fell back into ripple after ripple. Because of the movement—forward and back and yet neither one—we watched the painting accordion in on itself, dissolving in ocher shadows.

Unfortunately, there was little time left. Being "cutters," Lenore and I had a limited, three-hour excursion. I urged her to follow me to the van Gogh exhibition. There, I was annoyed by a comment we overheard. A woman said, "You can see his psychosis developing here—poor thing." She was referring to drawings done in Arles, in which leaves twisted, seeming to grow in front of us—as if the sun had shaped each pen stroke. I couldn't believe anyone was that blind and stupid. Worse yet, I worried the comment would hurt Lenore, who supposedly had psychotic episodes.

"Look," I said, pointing to my watch. "There's a short cut to the exit—through a Japanese village set for a tea ceremony."

"Tea?" Lenore asked, a wisp of hair veiling her left eye and cheek.

"It's Buddhist. There's a trickling fountain."

As soon as we entered, she heard something else, "Listen. Ghosts hissing! Priests chanting for the dead ...." She turned to me and said that when she heard voices alone in the dark, they felt like songs swimming through her body. She claimed they were scouring the evil from her. Disturbed, I went silent and nodded politely. I had denied the severity of her illness, telling myself the others were wrong about her—they didn't understand Lenore's intuitive intelligence. But these statements were a glimpse into that horrifying world that tormented and tyrannized her—one whose sway was stronger than reason or friendship. We crunched across the stone path and made our way out of the museum.

On the bus, I stared through the window, watching buildings flash by as we headed toward the Toot. I was grieving, desperately trying to deny how disconcerting her statements were. Maybe I'd misunderstood, and she was pretending. Maybe the whole thing was a fantasy, which we both loved. But I knew better. The realization sank into my stomach.

Lenore asked, "You think that lady's gotten down the stairs?"

"I dunno. Maybe she never will."

"So … she's trapped?"

"I wish she weren't, but now I think she is," I said.

"That's so sad."

We arrived at 49th Street, left the bus, and passed through the entrance of the stone wall. Dinner had just been served. Animated chatter filled the dining room—something about a musical performance to be held at the Toot. Lenore excused herself before dessert. I knew something was terribly wrong and asked if she was okay.

She smiled and said, "Of course." I knew that wasn't true but didn't want to tell the nurses, risking our friendship. She had shared her experiences in confidence, because we'd gotten close. On the other hand, I wanted to intervene, to save her from herself. I was afraid those "voices" would encourage her to take her life, and it would be my fault. Anxiety clouded my thinking—I wasn't sure what to say and whom to say it to. Cora would have been the obvious person, but she was caught up with other patients. I didn't want to draw attention to Lenore's plight. But if she died, I'd never forgive myself. Confused and overwhelmed, I shut down, unable to think at all.

I stayed in the Day Room with other patients. Cora asked if we wanted to play Monopoly, engrossed in a seemingly endless game. I headed back to my room but couldn't get Lenore out of my mind. I understood wanting to die but couldn't fathom her hearing voices at night. Shrieking and taunting, they demanded that she butcher herself—orders she had to obey. I wanted to protect her from them while the rest of us slept. Picturing *her* descending the staircase into the mouth of hell, I tossed and turned for hours, finally falling asleep—only to have nightmares.

Three a.m.: shouts and commotion. An ambulance wailed above the whirr of the heating system. Disoriented, I ran into the hall, smelled the disinfectant, and saw the wet linoleum leading in a path to Lenore's room—the door ajar. Because she'd been bandaged and trundled off to the physical hospital, it was impossible to console her.

"Another five minutes and she woulda gone brain dead. Good thing we were doin' our rounds," a nurse said.

"Poor baby, right through the artery—maybe even a tendon," the other nurse said.

It was as if Lenore had performed surgery on herself. Had I only intervened, I could have stopped it from happening. I don't know what made me go inside Lenore's room—I had to. Clown posters collaged the wall beside her bed. I needed to see them to be comforted. But on all their happy, red-and-yellow faces, she had painted screaming mouths with her own blood. It dripped down the wall, like collective weeping. Nauseated, I bolted from her room and puked into my toilet.

I needed someone, anyone to talk to. I couldn't stay alone, so I went to the Day Room and sat on the Naugahyde couch. I kept picturing Lenore, her mouth replaced by a bleeding clown-mouth. No one else was in the lounge, but the light from the nurse's station was comforting. Even though I couldn't hear them through the glass, I saw the two nurses laughing. How dare they?

Surely they knew what had just happened to my friend. If they had half a heart, they'd be distraught. But I had long ago given up thinking that most of the employees cared about us. The Toot was just their job. We were some oddities they had to put up with. I waved to the nurses, but they didn't notice. I considered going up to them, to see if there was a resident on duty I could speak to, but I was growing increasingly furious. Unlike Cora, these nurses were insensitive monsters. I was afraid if I got near them, I'd heave a chair through the glass. Frightened by my growing rage, I ignored them. For all I knew, they thought Lenore's condition was funny. That would be more than I could bear.

I'd lost someone who was more than a friend. Although we had no romantic feelings for each other, she was like a part of me. I could no longer deny how sick she was. And any hope of getting control over my own life was seeping away like her painted blood.

Desperate, I took matters into my own hands. I didn't care if I died. Having pawned my flute to a friend of Al's weeks before, I'd bought works and half a bag of smack. I'd hidden it in the drop ceiling in case I needed it. I climbed on a chair, poked the ceiling tile up, grasped the syringe, spoon, and the packet of white powder. In my bathroom, I heated the mixture and shot it into my left arm. My drab room became iridescent. My grief dissolved into elation. Lenore appeared before me, smiled, turned into light, and then evaporated.

CHAPTER 23
COLD TURKEY

The next day, I had a session with Archibald. I tried to convey my grief about Lenore but couldn't finish my sentences. I was too disoriented and too much in pain. A stabbing sensation knifed through my stomach, as if I'd eaten something rancid. Rubbing my belly, I told him about the ache, saying a nurse had given me a spoonful of some medicine, which had no effect. He asked why my speech was slurred. I said I was tired, having slept badly after Lenore was taken away. Dr. Archibald then did something he'd never done before—he got up abruptly, walked over to me, pried my eyelids open, and peered into my eyes. "What I assumed—they're constricted," he said.

"What?" I asked, pretending not to understand. But my body was giving me away. My arms were itchy, and I scratched them. He slid back my sleeves and saw the tracks amid scabs from earlier cuts. I thought the tracks were barely noticeable, but he recognized what they were. The alarm showed on his face.

"How are you breathing?" he asked.

I didn't answer, unsure of what he wanted to hear. But I was out of breath just sitting there.

"Dear God, you've been shooting heroin. How many times?"

I couldn't believe it was so obvious. Humiliated, I didn't make eye contact. "Three, four, maybe five? Don't remember."

"Who gave it to you?"

I couldn't rat on Al and get him in trouble. "No one you know," I lied. I broke into tears and couldn't continue talking except to mumble, "Sorry."

He got on the phone and spoke to a nurse whose specialty was helping addicts to detoxify from heroin. Then he made another call to housekeeping. Orderlies were to search my room for paraphernalia. They found the burnt spoon. I told them where to look in the drop ceiling: I'd stashed the works and half of a bag of smack. Archibald said that, although I showed early signs of addiction, it was still mild. He explained that an adolescent brain, not fully formed, gets addicted more quickly. In such cases, he was against the use of replacement medication, further polluting my system. The benefit of going "cold turkey" was that I'd avoid creating another addiction. I'd be alone in my room for a day or two, with a family member by my side and the addiction nurse checking in on me regularly. An orderly appeared and escorted me back to the ward, as if I didn't know how to get there. The nurse made sure I drank lots of water and broth, saying she'd sit with me until my father arrived. My mother hadn't answered her phone, but he was at his office on Broad Street. As soon as he got the news, he left for the day. He showed up in twenty minutes.

I hoped he'd hug me and say he was worried. Instead, he asked, "Proud of yourself?"

Shivering, I muttered, "It's got nothing to do with pride."

"Should say not."

"I never did stuff like this before," I said. It felt like a meat cleaver sawed back and forth inside my stomach.

"I thought you knew me, Dad." Despite lying under two blankets, I shivered. The nurse had left a stack of them. My father laid another one over me.

"My stomach hurts!"

"The nurse said that'll pass." He changed the wet washcloth on my forehead. "I knew the nice kid I drove to Friday-night dance classes at your junior high. That's who I knew."

It must've looked like I was crying, but I wasn't—couldn't stop my eyes from tearing. "I'm still that boy," I said. But I was never certain who Dad was. Sure, he drove me to those dances, helped me spell complicated words, worked out equations, and even took long walks with me when I got upset over homework. But then that man abandoned me—replaced by someone who said I sickened him, who ridiculed my artistic talent, who excluded me from activities. I'd grown used to his unpredictable moods, as I had grown used to Mom's. But she never shunned or degraded me. As a son who was wasn't much of a boy, I learned that his revulsion was what I deserved. Other people treated me that way, too. But all of that shame melted when Dad's kinder side came back. How I yearned for it. My extreme behavior, which I couldn't have dreamt of two years earlier, coaxed that kinder side out. Maybe he was acting out of guilt, but I was grateful to see that part of him, no matter what it took.

"At those dances, you reminded me of myself when I met your mother."

"Must hurt to think about that now."

"Because we're divorced?"

Drenched under the blankets, I was mute. Talking was irritating.

"You think that means we don't still love each other?" he asked.

"Wasn't that kinda the point?" I managed to say.

"No, we just couldn't make it work."

I kept shivering. As he unfolded yet another blanket and spread it over me, I vomited into the bedpan. He held it. Spasms cut across my legs.

"You didn't do drugs back then?"

"No, not even cigarettes … God, this pain!" I puked again.

"It's going to take some time for the crap to work its way out of your system."

"I drank those little whisky bottles from airplanes," I said. "Some kid had them."

"Innocent enough," Dad said.

"But the booze felt harsh in my throat, like swallowing a Christmas tree." Talking about it added to my nausea. It was so severe I couldn't imagine it ever going away.

"What about that attractive blonde girl?"

"Drugs? No way."

She was my brother's age. She had short hair and wore long, hand-made earrings. Having her own car, she offered escape from my family. When she came over, we'd drive to Riverton to go to the art cinema. We watched English movies with rock stars and countercultural types. After the movies, we drove to Lakeview Cemetery to watch the swans in moonlight, gliding under the stone bridge. In reflection, it formed a circle. We talked for hours. She knew so much, even about sexual things. But she never put the make on me. Yet, from my parents' point of view, we seemed to be dating. It was a perfect façade. She told me that someday when she married, *she'd* wear the tuxedo and the groom would wear a dress, which I thought showed how rebellious she was. But then she laughed, saying she'd never marry. She was a lesbian. I was surprised by her bold admission, not really sure what it meant.

Staring at the lake, I pointed out how awkward the swans looked out of water. They had clumsy, tar-colored feet and waddled more exaggeratedly than ducks. But in water, where they belonged, they were perfect. She and I agreed we were like them; we needed to find a place to fit in.

Perhaps out of disappointment, Dad didn't respond to what I told him about the girl he'd hoped I was dating. He asked, "How're you feeling?"

"Like the worst flu ever," I said, twisting my body over the side of my bed in an attempt to puke again. Nothing. Just choking, dry heaves, and a sour taste I couldn't get out of my mouth, despite chewing on gum. Every half hour, the nurse returned to empty the bedpan and take my temperature. When she did, I jolted, thinking she was going to hurt me. She reminded me that panic was one of the symptoms. It would pass.

Dad sat with me the entire day I spent sequestered in my room, applying wet washcloths to my forehead. I thought of the ones I'd soaked for Phil.

"I could've made sense of my thoughts, but no one let me," I said.

"No one *what*?"

"I had dreams about a wizard with colored sticks. Each one was a quality."

"Dean, that doesn't make any sense. Dr. Archibald has said you're euphoric. You understand what that means?"

"Is it something bad?"

"It means you live in a fantasy world."

"So?"

"In this world, you're a fifteen-year-old kid hooked on heroin." And then he made that gesture I associated with him: He buried his face in his hands as if he were trying to wipe it away. I couldn't tell if he was crying. I hoped he was.

"Sorry ... really, really sorry," I said, after thinking it all this time. Sorry for living, sorry for getting more and more sick of life. *Lenore was brave*. But I knew some young people were happy. My parents must've been like that. I pictured their youth, the way I watched old movies. When my father excused himself to eat (the thought of food made me gag), I thought back on what Mom had told me about meeting Dad. Comforted to think of a time before I was born, I slipped into her memories:

Big Band dances took place on the roof of the McBurney Y, the Empire State Building glowing in the distance. My mother went with her best friend. Boys stood on one side, girls on the other—couples dancing the Lindy Hop.

Mom later told her mother how much fun she'd had. But her strict mother said her daughter only wanted to rub up against the boys. My grandmother suggested a more wholesome alternative—a church picnic in Central Park.

The Great Lawn was parched and dusty. A boy stared in Sofia's direction. Certain her best friend was more desirable, my mother looked down. Minutes later, he was standing before the two girls. He drew a handkerchief from his jacket, knelt down, and wiped the dust from Sofia's patent-leather shoes. He said a girl so beautiful shouldn't have dust on her shoes. I loved playing that scene over in my mind. Then I couldn't help feeling sad that those young lovers would eventually grow to hate each other.

My father returned and emptied the stainless steel bedpan. The stench was awful.

"Dad, can I ask you a question 'bout Mom?"

"Depends."

"Did you date?" I said.

"Movies mostly. She loved Bing Crosby."

"Then?'

"I got accepted to SMU and asked her to marry me. Couldn't believe she said yes."

"In Dallas?"

"Yes, it helped your mother get away from her sister."

My eyes started tearing beyond my control.

"You see me as some stoic monster," he said.

I looked up, unable to deny I felt that way.

"Well, I'm not," he said. "Sometimes, when no one's around, I go to church to cry."

Struck by how similar we were, I was overcome by regret: that we'd never really known each other, that our family was built on opposing alliances, putting me at odds with him. I wanted to love him but didn't know how. I thought the best way to start would be to share something private, "Dad, you understand paradoxes?"

"Such as?"

"I wish I had faith, but I don't. So I prayed for it."

"I pray, too."

"Does it help?" I asked.

"Sometimes it's all I have. You have no idea how alone I get."

"Like when you said nobody would come to your funeral?" After another dry heave, I wiped my mouth and whispered, "Maybe we're alike."

The dinner bell rang. "Listen, Dean, the nurse said you should try to put *something* in your stomach—even toast. I have to go home." He hugged me, promised he'd come back soon, and disappeared. I didn't want him to leave. It was the first time we'd spoken so honestly. As he hugged me, I froze. I didn't want him to see how crushed I was, how much I wanted him to stay. My conditioning to be tough prevented me from letting him know I loved him—conditioning I'd learned from *his* example.

I toweled off and walked to the ward for the first time that day. Reaching the dining room, I was silent. A blurry sensation pushed through my body. Everything got on my nerves: the dissonant sound of the TV and its canned laughter, somebody arguing with a nurse, the smell of greasy food. Dad's words played in my head like a confusing static. After picking at a dinner roll, I drifted back to my room.

An idea flashed through my thoughts. Although orderlies had confiscated the spoon, the works, and what was left of the heroin, they had not found the last syringe. I'd hidden a second one behind the radiator. The more I engaged in drugs, the more devious I'd become. It was my way of fighting back.

I had a plan that didn't involve drugs.

It would stop the pain, once and for all.

CHAPTER 24
THREE POSSIBILITIES

Air. Pure air.

Why not shoot *that* into my vein? I'd overheard kids say, if injected, it travels straight to the heart, killing instantly. That snippet of conversation floated back to me as the only option left.

Furious heat took over. I tied the rubber strap to my left arm, filled the cylinder of the syringe with air, slid the needle into my bulging vein, shoved the plunger in.

Tears blurred my vision, but my crying dissolved as I watched, calmly waiting for relief. *Soon, it'll be over.* The lump burrowed under the skin of my left arm like a mole, hurting as it tunneled its way to my shoulder, then disappeared. Nothing! I wasn't even lucky enough to get it to kill me.

The heat returned—pulsing, devouring my ability to think. I drew more air into the syringe chamber, punctured my vein, jammed the plunger all the way. *This time for sure.* Another lump squirmed up my left arm. More pain. The swelling disappeared as it reached my shoulder. Again, nothing. By this time the urgency had vanished, replaced by more tears. I couldn't see.

Then: frailty.

Then: blankness.

Then: overwhelming remorse.

I rolled my sleeve down to cover my bloody arm, ran out of my room, away from myself, into the world of people. Matthew happened to be in the hall, book in hand.

"Please, ya gotta protect me!"

"Who the hell's after you, Dean?"

"My room."

He followed me in. I rolled up my sleeve. "What in God's name?" he said.

"Air … tried … shooting. Wanted—"

"Slow down. You what?"

"A second time." I hugged him, saying, "Sorry, Da—" I started to say *Dad* but caught myself. Matthew held me, patting my back. Pulling away, I protested, "But I don't. Don't want it anymore. Please protect me." After the second failed attempt, another force—the will to survive—sprang back, stronger than my desire to off myself. I didn't know I still had that will inside me, but I knew in my gut I had to cling to it. I was afraid to be alone, where I might give in to suicidal thoughts again.

Matthew opened my door, gestured to a nurse, whispering something to her. Three solemn-looking aides seemed to materialize from nowhere. They strapped me to a gurney and whisked me off to a medical doctor. Matthew remained by my side the whole time. Cora, seeing the commotion, rushed over. She stroked my forehead. It seemed silly—I could walk. Were they afraid I'd faint?

The doctor explained an air embolism, as he called it, could have ended up in one of three possible destinations: my heart, resulting in a heart attack. My brain, causing a stroke. Or my lungs, where it would be absorbed. He said the chance of the air being soaked up by my lungs was one in a million. For it to have happened a second time was nothing short of a miracle. He told me he said that as a nonreligious man. "You came very, very close to a horrible end. I hope you know how lucky you are," he said.

Even though I couldn't answer, his words hammered into my head. I couldn't make eye contact with him, looking down, trying to make sense of my feelings. I couldn't tell if what he said was true or just meant to scare me from trying this again. Whatever the reality, his warning worked. Then a realization hit: I'd lost the faith once learned at my grandmother's altar. The year and a half at the Toot had pulverized it. But just weeks before I'd prayed to believe in God again. To survive my suicide attempts was a double blessing: a life saved, a faith renewed.

My grandmother believed in miracles. She said they had to be appreciated by the people who received them; otherwise, their effect was lost. I had to grab this opportunity. I might not get a second one. As I tried to take in how lucky I was, I pushed away wanting to kill myself with all my mental strength.

It wasn't without a fight. Part of me didn't believe the doctor had told the truth about the three possibilities. That nagging cynicism bugged me. But I blocked it from my thoughts. I didn't care if what he told me was accurate or not—it was true for me. It was like finding solid ground. No one could budge me from it, not even myself. I made a new vow: I would never try suicide again.

Unfortunately, no one knew that but me. I had to deal with the consequence of my attempts. An aide escorted me to I.C.U. Earlier, getting sent there would've seemed like an achievement. This time, I became obedient. A nurse redressed my wound, took my blood pressure and temperature. Finally, she asked me to take my clothes off (they could be torn and used as a noose), adding I could leave my underwear on. After putting my clothes in a locker, she handed me a synthetic blanket that couldn't be torn. I wrapped it around me like a robe.

Cora knocked on my door, carrying chocolate pudding in a Styrofoam bowl with a plastic spoon. She looked uneasy. "Pudding, Dino?"

"Thanks, Cora."

"You're going to be okay. Dr. Archibald's coming."

"It's after nine," I said.

"Dino, you could have died."

For the next hour, she and I spoke as I slowly ate the pudding, licking the spoon. I was surprised to enjoy the taste of food again. A few minutes before ten, Archibald stuck his head into the cell, grinning. I couldn't figure out why he looked so cheerful. It annoyed me.

"May I come in?"

I said, "Cora was—"

"Leaving. I didn't want our friend to be alone," she said.

I asked, "See you tomorrow, Cora?"

"You know the answer to that, Dino." I watched her flatten her pilled wool scarf before draping it around her neck, crisscrossing it, pulling one side up, and exposing its paisley flower. She slid on her coat and smiled goodbye. Like the lilt of her accent and her lavender perfume, her gestures had a comforting graciousness.

"What do you think of your new hotel accommodations?" Archibald asked.

Biting my lower lip, I blurted, "Ugly."

"Dean, what happened?"

I glared at him. Picking at a splotch of paint on the mat, I asked, "Couldn't they clean this place?"

"What's going on?"

"*It*," I spat.

"Dean, what are you talking about?"

"*It!*"

"What?"

"That feeling—can't say more than that."

"Don't think. Just finish this: I want to hurt myself when I feel like. . . ."

"A huge, ugly mistake I can't erase."

"Well, I'm certainly happy you failed to erase yourself."

"Me too," I said.

Dr. Archibald seemed frightened for the first time.

"I was so sick and Dad was really nice."

"And?" Archibald said.

"I felt bad about what a mess—"

Dr. Archibald sat down beside me and did something that should have bothered me but didn't—he caressed my shoulder. Afraid of what my eyes might say, I didn't look at him, my heart thumping. I liked it.

"Can't think. Maybe I *did* erase something," I mumbled. I broke down in a cascade of half-choked words. He lifted his hand from my shoulder. I missed its warmth. Comforting myself by rocking, I said, "I want … I really want … to live."

His eyes glossed over. For the first time, I realized he cared about me.

We sat there quietly for at least ten minutes before I could talk again. Picking at the paint, I said, "The doctor told me about the three ways the air could've gone. Was he right?"

"You're an *exceedingly* lucky young man."

"Now, I sort of believe in … living."

"No one would be happier to believe that than I, but you do realize I have to put you on suicide watch."

"I get it."

You'll sleep here and go back to the unit for Morning Meeting."

"I guess I won't—"

"No grounds privileges for weeks. I can't even begin to talk about excursions."

I kept picking at the paint.

"Oh, and another thing—your room's been stripped to make sure you haven't hidden anything else that's dangerous."

"Good," I said.

"Are you placating me?"

"No, it's like I stepped into a different room inside my head."

"Well, time will tell," Archibald said.

"Sorry I made you leave your house."

He smiled and left.

The following morning, my suicide attempts were the topic of discussion at Morning Meeting. Asked how I was feeling, I said I was happy to be back in my room. The I.C.U. mat had been uncomfortable. Glasses asked if I wanted to say something about the "in-ci-dent." I said I preferred discussing it with Archibald. She backed off.

The discussion then moved to Lenore. She was still in the medical hospital, where her wounds were healing.

Because her family could no longer afford to keep her at the Toot, she'd be transferred to a state mental institution about an hour from Philly. Glasses told us Matthew could drive a bunch of kids to visit her the following month.

Chambliss, David, Terri, Lion Boy, and I decided we had to go. And even though my excursion privileges had been revoked, Archibald bent the rules. Reasons: Matthew was joining us, and I had become a model patient since my suicide attempts.

I wanted to bring Lenore something. While reading each other's poems, she and I had loved eating chocolate sandwiches. So, I fixed her two of them. But unlike the ones we used to make—from Hershey's milk chocolate and any available bread—these had to be top quality. I wedged slabs of bittersweet chocolate into sourdough bread. Glasses had gotten the ingredients for me. I asked one of the ladies in the kitchen to warm the treats in the oven, to make the chocolate melt.

I considered bringing Lenore a poem I'd recently written, comparing her to Ophelia (Matthew had been teaching us *Hamlet*), but realized it wasn't a positive message. Instead, I brought her a clover necklace I'd made from the grounds where we used to read.

As Matthew's old car sputtered toward the state mental hospital, James Taylor's song "Fire and Rain" came on the radio. It always made me think of her. I was struck by the ugliness of the concrete buildings—grimmer than any prison. We drove closer, and I noticed there were iron bars, not grills, on all the windows.

We couldn't go in, so an aide summoned Lenore. She finally opened the door, looking out, as though not recognizing us. It was hard to talk above other patients' screams. Their howling didn't sound real—more like the recorded screeches in funhouses. A look—both surprised and horrified—had reshaped her forehead. With a medicated smile, she said, "So nice you came." She had become a wraith, her face erased like those in her drawings. Where was my friend? As much as I wanted to pretend she could get better, I realized nothing I could ever do or say would stop the hellish voices from coaxing her over that dark ravine inside her head. In that moment, I saw her falling—forever out of my reach. I lost her. Although I was mourning, I couldn't risk letting her pull me down with her—not after having chosen to live. My resolve was even stronger than guilt.

Hoping she wouldn't notice the sadness in my eyes, I handed her the sandwiches and hung the clover chain around her neck, saying, "I miss you. We all do, even the people who couldn't come." She could barely bend her arm to take the sandwiches. The surgical dressing was thick and stiff, running from her wrist to her bicep like a cast. Cora hugged Lenore, telling her how pretty she looked. Lion Boy stroked her hair. Matthew assured her we'd visit again.

But we never did.

CHAPTER 25
THAW

After a relentless winter, shoots started pushing up from the soil. Lenore said they looked like green rhinoceros horns. She had pointed out a snail inching without its shell, a pigeon's iridescent neck. Losing her left me with a hollow ache like having a lung removed. I'd never again wander the grounds with her, seeing things through her eyes.

I hoped Dr. Archibald would help. Since my recent suicide attempt, I'd come to trust him more. I walked outdoors to the Old Building to get to his office and knocked on the door.

"Don't stand on ceremony," he said, motioning for me to enter.

I gathered my words: Even though Lenore and I weren't boyfriend and girlfriend, I was grieving her loss. Seeing her in the state institution made it worse. He assured me it was a reputable facility, where she'd get good care. For all I knew, it was affiliated with the Toot. Without expressing my cynicism, I asked if she'd ever be cured. He said no, but with appropriate medication, she could lead a normal life. He promised—once released from our institutions—that she and I could be friends again. I wanted to let myself believe it, knowing it was a lie.

He said the buds outdoors affirmed renewal, and the trees were brimming with sap. He then warned me not to let mine build up. Reminding me he was also a medical doctor, he said to let it "flow." I was tired of all his masturbation talk, hoping he'd be bored of it, too. No such luck. I wanted to jump out of my skin, across the desk, and choke him. I did have sexual feelings, but mine were the kind no one wanted to hear. Most kids were lucky. Boys had girlfriend problems; girls, boyfriend problems. Just about every song was about *that*. But worse than feeling alone—I was tormented.

I knew how adults showed one side, only to snap back into another—some sadistic game. My parents had done that, Dad more so. Years earlier, I'd overheard him say I sickened him. Between being bullied and the male-sex fantasies I couldn't rip from my mind, I sickened *myself*.

And here I was, sitting across from a man who never tired of taunting me with sex. It was either a form of entrapment, or he was excited by me. If that was true, he was stuck in a situation worse than mine. His own profession called homosexuality a mental disorder. If he did feel tortured, he put on a good front.

I had to embarrass him. I pointed to a bronze figurine on his shelf—a satyr with a large erection—and asked why he hid it when my parents visited. He made his garden-party chuckle, saying it was a fertility spirit. Another chuckle. He described how Ancient Greeks encouraged intimate relationships between men and boys. A weird flush came over me. I had to stifle my rage. He'd figured me out but not to offer the support and guidance I needed. As if seeing through me, he knew my sexual fantasies were about men. Archibald was trying to expose what I had hidden from everyone, including myself. I stared into his eyes and said, "What do you mean?"

He told me mentors helped the "ephebes" to mature. The youths were growing, mentally and physically. (I wanted to be anywhere else—looking out the window, hoping to see Peggy.) He said teenage boys sometimes *develop* rather suddenly. They can be uncomfortable in their new bodies and need an adult's advice. I never had anyone to talk to about sex. I wished I could have spoken to Archibald about my desires, but being the "H" word was worse than having crazy-germs.

Terrified that he was trying to coax the truth out of me, I changed the topic. The unit was noisier than usual—patients playing rock albums at top volume. I asked if some policy could get kids to turn their record players down. He said rules existed, but the staff had difficulty enforcing them. Fed up, I told him I had a clay sculpture in the kiln at O.T. and needed to take it out before it exploded.

It *had* been noisy on the unit. However, the next week Al went off to Texas. He'd be back after Easter. His friends had flown off to visit their families. It was like spring break. Since going cold turkey, I stayed clear of Al. I didn't want to fall under his influence. He'd found other hangers-on to do his "errands."

I had a session with both shrinks two days later. I noticed the satyr had disappeared and that Archibald never talked about man-boy relationships in front of anyone but me. I wanted to report his comments, but no one would have believed me. After all, he was the director of the adolescent unit.

Mandrill said, "We've been reviewing your case. It appears the syringe incident was a turning point."

I nodded my head.

"Everybody—from the O.T. staff to Cora—has seen a marked improvement."

"Cora?" I asked.

"She cares about you, Dean," he said, as if doling out some state secret.

"We've officially reinstated your excursion privileges," Archibald said.

"Really?" I was thrilled.

"You've exhibited significant progress," he said.

"Do my parents know?"

"They're picking you up tomorrow," he said.

Mom showed up the following day in a new car, driving us to what had been our house. After being in the Toot for almost two years, it came as a shock to be allowed back to my childhood home—despite the divorce. Dad was still living there. Mom had moved to an apartment near the Philadelphia Museum of Art, but she came back to spend the holiday with us. We'd all celebrate Orthodox Easter—when even the most irreligious Greeks go to church. Although our lives had been altered forever, the house looked the same.

The charade of being an intact family seemed important to everyone, acting out roles that never existed: the harmonious, adoring parents and kids, gathered for a holiday. This playacting underscored the opposite. But my parents kept up the Hallmark façade, as if I should forget what really happened. The angry part of me wanted to scream, *You're all insane!* But the nice-boy part of me, the one who patched things up, knew this farce helped them feel less guilty. I kept the angry side quiet, even though he was aching to tell them they had destroyed our family.

My mood changed when I entered my bedroom, with my beloved radio and cat. This was where I'd grown up, slept, studied, and tried to hang myself. As if neither Bakely Academy nor the Toot had ever happened, my cat still waited for me. When I approached him, he purred loudly. I hugged him, his white fur sticking to my face. Pressing my cheek into his side, I wondered if I'd ever loved a person that much.

Mom and Dad slept in separate rooms. The next day, they spoiled me, taking me shopping. It was kind of an apology, but I enjoyed it. Later that night, I changed into a dark jacket and yellow tie, sleeking my hair into a ponytail for midnight Mass. My church-averse family enjoyed that service for its drama. We drove to Saint Thomas Greek Orthodox Church in Cherry Hill. Our plan: arrive at eleven-fifteen, buy candles, and get a seat at the end of the pew for a quick escape. The services are so long that many Greeks, unless very religious, come late and leave early.

I hadn't seen Phillip since Puerto Rico. I had kept his grotesque secret and wondered if he was still injecting drugs. I doubted he knew I'd done it, also. But somehow, *my* having shot heroin made me feel less guilty about him. I was no longer the model son—no longer depriving Phil of happiness and success. Communication had ceased between us. Maybe that was why he didn't visit. Guilt, reflecting both ways, had solidified into a barricade of ice. I felt responsible for keeping his secret. He (I hoped) felt bad about the incident itself. The less we talked, the less we *could* talk.

His jet-black hair wisped across his brow, a jacket engulfing his lanky frame. He and my parents bought candles and entered the sanctuary, saving me a seat. I approached the icons to pray. A sinner, I was afraid of Jesus. But the Virgin Mary was both mother and friend. I then slid into the pew next to my family. Mom wore a straw hat edged in black grosgrain. Light filtered through the brim, casting a crosshatch pattern on her face. One by one, the lights clicked off.

We sat in the pitch black, silent except for a man clearing his throat. Symbolizing the defeat over death, the priest bellowed, "Come receive the light from the unwaning Light!" I, too, had defeated death, choosing never to try suicide again. The priest dipped his fire toward two men with tall tapers. Candle by candle, a glow grew throughout the congregation.

"Sweetheart, do you have singles?" Mom asked.

Men pushed long-handled baskets through each pew, collecting money. Like us, very few congregants came the rest of the year. Clutching our candles, we swarmed toward the exit and the chilly night air.

As I passed a gaggle of elderly women, they squawked, "Look at his hair!"

"Look up there!" I rhymed, pointing to frescos of Old Testament patriarchs and even Jesus himself—all sporting shoulder-length hair. Proud of how I dealt with their rudeness, I followed my family. In our car, we guarded the flames, submerged in their amber light. We kept the fires lit till getting out of the car, when the wind blew them out.

I wondered how Mom must've felt, returning to a house that stood as a monument to her failed marriage. I took comfort in knowing she'd filed for divorce and was free of my father and brother. Where did I fit in?

Inside, the feast she'd prepared awaited us. It was to have followed a day-long fast. In my family, where psychiatry had replaced religion, we bypassed the fast, enjoying the feast. Waiting for Mom to ladle out *mayeritsa* soup, and for Dad to carve the garlic-studded lamb, Phil and I played an Easter game. A bowl of red eggs sat on the table. Each player smacks an egg, point to point, then flat-side to flat-side, each time affirming the Resurrection. One egg breaks; the other doesn't. It's not unusual to trounce two or three. Beyond that, it's rare. Phil's egg had smashed each one.

"Phil, why are you covering the egg with your hand?" I said.

"Strengthening the sides."

Quick, I tossed him a piece of bread. His reflex was to catch it and drop the egg, which, it turned out, was made of plaster. But I couldn't be angry; it reminded me of his boyhood pranks. We laughed about it over dinner. Afterwards, Dad and Phil excused themselves. I helped Mom with the dishes.

The following morning, she knocked on my door, peeking in, "Sweetheart, you've gotta go back after lunch." I wanted to believe we'd magically been given a second chance to have the family I'd always dreamed of. Somehow, pretending like I had a home—even though I no longer did—made me dread going back to reality. I considered hiding in a part of the attic only Phil and I knew about, but it would only prolong the inevitable.

Dad and my brother watched a baseball game on TV. Noticing me pass by, Phil asked if I wanted help packing. I mouthed, "No, thanks," disappearing into the basement, where I took my clothes from the dryer and packed my suitcase.

I needed Mom to know I cherished our alliance. She was preparing lunch in the kitchen, where we'd shared our deepest thoughts. I asked if she needed help. She said no, so I sat at the table. I spotted the clay swan I'd sculpted as a boy, its neck cracked and glued. The baby swans on her back had disappeared.

"What happened?" I said.

She told me she didn't know how the figurine had broken. She'd found it in the attic swathed in toilet paper, the little ones loose. Adding glue, she thought they'd hold. After the divorce, the house had been repainted, the boxes moved. She shook her head. I told her at least the mother swan—the most important one—was okay.

"Dean, your omelet's ready. Eat and let's head back." During the drive, a wordless haze crept over me. I felt kidnapped and fantasized about bolting from the car, afraid of getting injured. As the vehicle purred through the entrance, I grabbed my suitcase, told Mom and Dad I loved them, and trudged inside.

At least I looked forward to seeing my friends. Most of the kids had returned, except for Al. Cora greeted us, starting a game of Clue. I eventually went back to my room to unpack and sleep.

Morning Meeting. Without asking us how our holidays had been, Glasses lowered her voice. She seemed to take perverse delight in imparting bad news: "There's been a tragedy during the Passover/Easter holiday. Alton Langland, 'Al' to most of you, is gone. He ... shot himself in the head with his father's gun. Died instantly. The wake and funeral will take place in Texas, but we're organizing a memorial at a horse trail he loved, where we can say our farewells."

I was stunned but also relieved. Around him, I was nobody. He had tapped incessantly on the wall, stealing sleep and my ability to organize my thoughts. Around him, I was a toy. He had used me to smuggle drugs. Around him, I became an addict. Worst of all was the realization that around him I chose to give myself away, to gain his approval—something unattainable. It was what I believed I needed. But had I gotten it, it still wouldn't have validated me. And he'd used a firearm— what I'd fantasized about and lived in fear of.

I didn't want to go to the memorial. But everyone else did, so I tagged along. Matthew drove us to the horse trail that had been a Lenni-Lenape burial ground. Hornbeam trees sheltered us from the sun.

We stood in a circle, each person eulogizing Al. One girl said he always sensed when she was sad and needed cheering up, and that he always found something funny to say. Chambliss (how *could* she?) said he was someone she could lean on. Then, one of the boys I never talked to addressed the gathering. I'd admired him from a distance, knowing he was smart. Having a hard time speaking, he said, "Al was the smartest fuckin' person I've ever known. He really *got* me. A true friend."

I was shocked, wondering if we'd known the same person. When my turn came, I said, "I don't want to say anything mean, but I can't say anything nice. I'm sorry he was suffering. I'm sorry, but I didn't like him. He made my life hell. Nobody would listen to my complaints when he was alive. Why should I lie now that he's dead?" I kept my eyes fixed on the ground to avoid others' reactions. I was not going to budge. Having the strength to say what I felt and believed was a new ability. It made me feel powerful for the first time in my life. And I liked it.

In the car ride, Glasses, to my amazement, told me she admired my honesty and courage. I had made a decision I believed in. A week passed. No one made me take back what I had said.

CHAPTER 26
THE EUMENIDES OF SEX

A dark mood poisoned the ward. Patients moped over Al's suicide, saying they hadn't seen it coming. I was baffled, which I kept to myself. Later, at Group, the session was devoted to his death. Even though I didn't want to participate in eulogizing him, I finally asked what no one else would, "Was he high when he did it?"

That silenced the room. We all knew it was true—even Glasses. It occurred to me that some of the grieving might have been a cover up for shared blame. He was a drug addict, given free rein to destroy himself. I knew what that looked like, having grown up with Phil. I had also been with Al when he used and trafficked drugs and saw how adults entrusted to care for him looked the other way. They were perpetrating the sham by ignoring these facts. I looked at Glasses and reminded her *she* was the one who'd reported his "illicit activities." The way I'd been honest at his memorial, I needed to be honest here, even if it meant being called "insolent," a word she and my father liked. I didn't know where my courage to be so blunt came from, but once the words flew out of my mouth, I waited for a harsh reaction. No one spoke. That said everything I needed to hear. Glasses cleared her throat and agreed there was some truth to what I had said. Looking at her watch, she dismissed Group early.

Terri walked me back to the ward, where lunch was about to be served. She said I had a "big mouth," which she admired. I remembered her standing up for me, saying things no one wanted to hear, things that could have resulted in her loss of privileges, but she did it anyway. I told her I'd learned how to speak up from her, and how it felt like survival. Finally, no one could ever erase me. She squeezed my shoulder.

After lunch, we headed to Matthew's class, where Chambliss said she kept having nightmares of Al's head exploding like a watermelon, like the footage of Kennedy's assassination.

Matthew said we could turn our suffering into writing. He had been teaching us about Greek mythology and the concept of transformation: The Furies would punish crimes, striking the offenders with insanity. But, as guardians of the law, they could change themselves into the life-affirming Eumenides. He saw them as symbolic; we could transform our anger and hurt into poems. He read us some famous elegies and said if our writing made us feel anything, good *or* bad, that was okay. He gave us permission to cry.

I had no tears.

Then he suggested it might make us feel better to fill our minds with something beautiful. He'd made plans to take us on another excursion: The Barnes Foundation in Merion, Philadelphia's exclusive Mainline. I'd heard of the museum before and knew they required reservations, allowing a fixed number of visitors each day. He said the Toot insisted that another staff member come along, so he'd invited Glasses. Combining her and Matthew was like mixing formaldehyde with milk.

Two days later, we arrived at the elegant sandstone mansion—one of the best collections of Impressionist art in the world. We wandered through room after room. Matthew talked at length about the Renoirs, Matisses, Seurats, and Monets. Glasses never said a word, feeling out of her league. It was satisfying to see her humbled.

I loved Matisse's patterns. I couldn't stop looking at *The Music Lesson*. A boy practiced the piano, being taught by his mother. The father read by himself. Another boy sat in a rocking chair whose legs resembled large, cursive C's. The painting reminded me of my family.

After leaving the museum, Matthew and Glasses took us to Chinatown. We stuffed ourselves. The restaurant must have doused the food with MSG, because when I got back to the Toot, I was drowsy and had to nap. The dinner bell woke me up. Over waxy lasagna, Terri said she'd thought more about our conversation. While she liked my honesty, she thought it best to offer positive thoughts to people who committed suicide. "It's a kind of a cycle, like karma."

"Terri, I do feel bad for him." Then pausing, I said, "Ever notice how *cycle* sounds like *psycho*?"

"Well, speakin' of psychos, a guy from another loony bin's comin' here."

"Is there some kind of nut-house fraternity? I asked. "Phi Delta Wacko?"

She laughed with her scratchy, Newport-Menthols voice. Both patients and staff preferred menthols, as if they were the official cigarettes of mental hospitals.

Terri said, "Boxer and me know each other from Boston."

"Boxer?"

"He's fuckin' beautiful—Italian and Cherokee."

"What's with that name?"

"He's sweet, but when he's pissed, he fights crazy."

"Scary," I said.

Terri said, "They straitjacketed him. Not sure why they're bringin' him *here*. These snake pits are all the same."

The next day at lunch, the gloom had been replaced by commotion among the patients—as if a rock star had arrived. When everyone finally sat down, I spotted Boxer. He had dark hair parted sloppily and full eyebrows arching over large, olive-black eyes. He was somewhere between stocky and muscular. A dizzying sensation pulsed through me. I tried to ignore it.

As I looked down to eat, he passed by my table. "Hi, Terri's told me a lot about you," he said directly to me.

"Really? It's nice to … meet you," I said not believing he'd look at, let alone talk to me. I couldn't make eye contact. The more I thought about him, the more flustered I became. The Furies of suicide had transformed into the Eumenides of sex. He laughed. I worried I'd made of fool of myself. I was a month shy of sixteen. Boxer was twenty, a man. Occasionally, he'd pass by my paintings at O.T., saying something complimentary, which excited *and* embarrassed me. I nodded—not sure what I was feeling, not sure what to say. My sexual fantasies about men were all replaced by him. I never allowed myself to attach that disgusting "H" word to my desires. "Homosexuals," a classmate had once told me, were very uncommon, maybe two or three in the whole world. All of them lived in filthy apartments near Times Square. They had unwashed hair, pasty skin, and molested little boys. The idea of being one of those vile creatures filled me with terror. Even if it meant lying, I had to uphold a positive image of myself, glued together by willpower.

The next day at O.T., I started another self-portrait. Peering into the mirror, I saw Chambliss, and swerved around. She stood there with a new patient: Leigh, an artist from Merion, near The Barnes Foundation. Chambliss gestured that she would finish showing Leigh around. I promised to see them at dinner. Engrossed in my project, I continued drawing until O.T. closed.

Back at the unit, I found Terri sobbing by the TV. Boxer, she managed to say, had suffered one of his violent episodes. He couldn't stomach people telling him what do to. I respected that. I didn't, however, condone his breaking a chair, smashing the glass of the nurses' station, and punching an aide. Orderlies had straitjacketed, sedated, and locked him in a padded cell in I.C.U.

"They're gonna hurt my baby!" Terri wailed. She told me no one understood how brilliant and kind Boxer was. She figured Glasses cared least of all because she was jealous, wanting him for herself. I never knew if Terri's comments about her were true. Before, I would have agreed. But having seen another side of Glasses, after the memorial and the recent Group session, I was less inclined to badmouth her.

"It's hard to imagine. He's got those beautiful, sad eyes," I said. Mortified to have uttered those words, I shut myself up.

As if she hadn't heard me, Terri vowed to visit Boxer later that night, to speak to him through the small grill at the door—like in a confessional. She knew he'd be Thorazined, unable to talk, and would soon conk out.

But a sympathetic nurse allowed her to stay in the I.C.U. lounge, where families waited. She'd be there to offer encouragement as soon as he woke in the morning.

When I took Thorazine, to come down from acid, I felt thick and distant for days, as though looking at everything through Plexiglas. That was after taking it only one time. I imagined a regular regimen of it being like a chemical lobotomy.

On the ward, gossip about Boxer filled everyone's conversation. His presence had shifted the focus from Al. Leigh, the new patient, floated over in a peasant skirt, getting the Boxer news from Terri. Unlike everyone else, however, Leigh cared little about the drama. She seemed to think it was beneath her.

Changing the subject, she told me she was going to Merion the following week to stay with her uncle. He was some famous novelist. She asked if I wanted to come, explaining he had a mansion with a pool, and the adults were too caught up with their parties and gin to care what kids did. It would be perfect—we'd get the "parental guidance" the Toot demanded and we'd have fun. Food, records, art supplies, and a pool. That reality shimmered in stark contrast to the Toot, Thorazine, and rubber rooms. My mind swung between looking forward to a getaway and craving a friendship with Boxer.

That night, Terri traipsed up to I.C.U., as stoic and long-suffering as Jacqueline Kennedy after the assassination. Chambliss, David, and I waited on the ward by the piano at the end of the hall. As though watching through the sight of a rifle, we fixed our eyes on the front door. Finally, it flew open. Terri dashed toward her room, mascara bleeding. We flocked to comfort her, which we knew she wanted.

"It's fuckin' awful what they've done to my baby," she whimpered as I stroked her forehead. Chambliss wiped her face with Kleenex. "He howls like he's in agony," Terri said. She honked her nose in the tissue. "They took his clothes away so he can't strangle himself."

I asked if she'd seen him naked, embarrassed to find that interesting at such a sad time. She said he was bloody too, from banging his head on the wall. Chambliss stayed with Terri after I left. Although patients weren't supposed to enter each other's rooms, we did it all the time. No one ever seemed to notice or care.

In my room, I fell asleep picturing him nude. I would've given anything to comfort him, to prove how much he needed me, as Terri was trying to do. Her feelings for Boxer exceeded friendship.

Because I wanted to free myself from the Toot's epidemic of suffering, Leigh's invitation drifted back into my thoughts. She had come into the Toot the way I had—not feeling like she belonged there, seeing it as temporary. Maybe that's why we became friends.

Unfortunately, Archibald had a field day with my female friendships. He asked if we had performed specific sexual acts, described in salacious detail. "Surely you fantasize about Leigh and Chambliss."

"Meaning?" I asked.

"Hormones, my boy. That phallus of yours must get rock hard." He paused and glared at my crotch. "Good, all this talk has you aroused."

The slightest provocation had that result—even riding a bus over a bumpy road. I learned to carry a magazine. I hated myself for letting *him* get me excited.

"I *am* a psychiatrist."

"Meaning?"

"Both mind and body need release. You can do it here. I have towels."

"Do *what*?" I never knew if he was serious or just trying to make me mad.

"You're so inhibited," he said.

"Listen, is this session over? I say it *is*." I found the courage to let him have it, picturing him embalmed, his skin leathery, encased in glass. I marched out of his office.

That didn't mean the sexual taunting, which both shrinks practiced, had stopped. About a week later, Dr. Mandrill decided we'd meet on the grounds. He wanted to hear about my masturbation fantasies. I tried to laugh it off, but he persisted, "Why are you embarrassed about something so natural?" he said.

"None of your business."

"Defensive, aren't we?" He laughed.

I picked up a heavy twig and hurled it at him.

"Ouch! You almost got me in the pecker." Bingo—my target. Instead of reporting me to security, he found my anger amusing, even worthy of respect. He never mocked me after that but did communicate the "incident" to Archibald, whom I saw the next day.

He said, "Are you emulating Boxer?"

I asked why I would want to *emulate* him, not entirely sure what that word meant. Archibald pointed out where the twig had hit Dr. Mandrill was not arbitrary. It was *significant*—another of his favorite words.

"You mean down there?" I said.

"It's called a *penis* or *phallus*, the word I prefer. You're old enough to speak about your own anatomy."

The way I was fed up with Group, I'd had it with Archibald's slimy comments. I decided to belittle him. He was wearing one gray sock and one blue one. Before, one had been black, another navy—an easier mistake. But this was so obvious. Was he less in control than he pretended? "Gee, Dr. Archibald, your socks are different colors again. That's pretty funny."

"Let's get back to the thrig ... twig-throwing incident."

"Oh, I'm violent 'cause I threw a twig at someone who tormented me?"

"Tormented?"

"That's right. How am *I* supposed to feel?"

"You know Dr. Mandrill and I ..."

I sensed from his voice he heard my frustration and even felt concern. I pointed out that his comparing me to Boxer was ridiculous. He would've done a lot worse than throwing a twig. More like a sharp rock.

"You are aware that Boxer is my patient?"

"Terri told me. We ... like him."

"How so?" His smile curled around the word "so."

Ignoring his question, I asked if Leigh was also his patient. He said yes and asked why I was interested. I said because she was an artist and had invited me to spend the following weekend at her mom's house. The woman would be there. He said he'd ask Leigh to get something in writing. I told him if I got the excursion, we'd go to the Barnes Foundation, which I thought would impress him. He made it clear that an apology to Mandrill was in order. Translation: if you want privileges, do this.

I said I'd apologize that day—crafty enough to get what I wanted, regardless of the bruises to my self-esteem.

L eigh and I waited at the Toot's entrance. When her mother's chauffeur honked the horn, we piled into the limousine. He drove us from West Philadelphia to Merion. Trees on both sides of the road met in the middle, forming a leafy tunnel. Past boxwood hedges, past estates, we pulled into a driveway, leading to a mansion with a mansard roof. We thanked the driver.

The screen door had a slash through it, bandaged with Scotch tape. No one met us. I wondered if we'd gotten the date wrong. Inside, stacks of yellowed newspapers made it hard to maneuver past worn furniture. A urine stink overpowered us. I heard the sound of a dog's unclipped claws on parquet, followed by a woman's high heels.

Leigh put on her adult voice, "Mother, this is my friend Dean."

Distracted, the woman said hello, expressed regret for the state of the house, and added it had been "pretty wild around here lately." She was sorry for not being able to spend more time with us but had to "take Uncle to the doctor." And then she said what people say when they're being unclear, "You know." I didn't know, but soon learned from Leigh that her uncle was an alcoholic, constantly in and out of rehab. Their lives revolved around his condition. As her mother got ready to leave, I tried to shake her hand but couldn't. She held the toy poodle with one, an amber-colored drink in the other.

Over the next two days, we glimpsed her and Uncle

only briefly. They were both embarrassingly polite. Then they seemed to evaporate. Leigh and I spent hours in the pool, playing our favorite albums on the turntable. She also had forty-fives. My favorite was *I Am the Walrus*. We'd place one record on the rubbery surface, with the arm pulled back, allowing the disc to play over and over and over. The music became a drug; we drew pictures to hypnotic songs, to undulating swoons of guitar and voice. Leigh had her own art room. I could have stayed there all weekend. Unlike the rest of the mansion, it was organized, the shelves labeled: *paper, canvases, pastels, pencils, oil paints, gouache.*

That night she cooked an Indian dinner, the most delicious, exotic thing I'd ever tasted—a curried, vegetarian dish. We ate with our fingers; she said that's what they do in India. A friend of her mother's, Sarala Ruth Pinto, was a sculptor in Center City. She had lived in a Hindu convent in California for three years and had been the cook for the nuns. "Sarala" was her Sanskrit initiation name. Leigh called her "Ruthie" and learned Indian cooking from her.

"She's eccentric," Leigh said, "which is why I love her. And get this—she always dresses in all white or all black. Wanna meet her?"

"Sounds cool," I said.

"She knew famous people in the forties, like Christopher Isherwood and Aldous Huxley. Y'know, *Brave New World*?"

"Oh, sure," I said, not wanting to seem stupid.

Ruth had stayed in a convent in Santa Barbara, the men in an ashram in Los Angeles. They met for lectures and services on Sundays with their guru, Swami Prabhavananda. Isherwood and his famous guru, Leigh told me, collaborated on a translation of the *Bhagavad Gita,* a sacred text. "Weird stuff—I totally get off on it," she said.

I'd never heard of those men and thought Hinduism was pagan, but I loved the fact that Ruth was an artist. "How are we gonna get there?" I said.

"The chauffeur. I'll call Ruthie and see if she's free tomorrow."

Later that night, Leigh and I slept in a guest room. We decided to stay together because I was spooked by the creaky house. I got ready and slipped into bed. Leigh undressed in front of me, making a point of taking off her panties and bending over to reveal her sex. She had been flirtatious earlier, by the pool. I was flattered but pretended not to notice. This was more blatant. Even though I'd "gone steady" with a girl in eighth grade, I'd never had real sex. I certainly wouldn't admit I was the "H" word, but I didn't want to have sex with Leigh. Worried about losing her friendship, I rolled over and acted as if I were asleep. I chose not to have sex with her the way I chose not to eulogize Al. I relished making my own decisions, given how rarely I'd been free to do that. This was the new Dean I had worked so long to create, the new self I thought I had lost. But here he was, emerging after I stopped trying to make him fit in to someone else's ideal. He had been a part of me all along.

Leigh and I woke late the following morning. Preparing to meet Ruth, we smoked some "quality" pot. I took only a couple of puffs. She promised it wasn't cut with other stuff, so I wouldn't hallucinate. Besides, it would be fun hearing all that mythology, about gods with animal heads and multiple arms, stoned.

The driver dropped us off on Delancey Street—a town house with a blue-gray door and white exterior. Leigh struck with the brass knocker: *clunk, clunk.*

Ruth opened the door, wearing a black miniskirt, black leotards, black turtleneck, black leather wristbands, and short, ankle-high boots—also black. She was a thin woman in her late forties, with long, straight hair. She either sported a dark tan or wore tanning makeup. She greeted us effusively, extended her hand to me, and said, "Leigh's told me wonderful things about you." Afraid of appearing high, I bowed my head as if in a foreign country.

Ruth led us past a polychrome horse from a nineteenth-century carousel. The living room had white brick walls. From the fireplace, a vase of eucalyptus leaves scented the air. Escorted into the den, we passed a large crucifix, which Leigh identified as Ruth's. It was a crucified Christ *without* a cross.

"Looks like he's flying," I said.

Leigh told me it was *modern* and that I should try to be more sophisticated.

"Dean's right," Ruth said, explaining she had depicted Christ freed from the constraints of the body. Some Hindus, she informed us, believe he was an avatar, and the body could not confine such a being. *Avatar,* I learned, was a Sanskrit word for someone like Buddha.

I said I drew people with fiery wings.

Ruth slid her glasses down her nose, revealing blue eyes

that burned like dry ice—appealing, yet intimidating. She was intrigued to find out I was an artist.

Suddenly, Leigh took pride in me and spoke on my behalf, saying I'd been a prodigy. She added I'd won a prize in an adult competition, at age seven.

"Is that true, Dean?"

"Yes, Mrs. Pinto."

"My husband and I would love to see your work."

I'd made a lot of new pieces at O.T. She asked me to call her a week later. Her husband, a painter, would finish his commission by then. She said the two of them were better critics as a pair. I stammered, telling her I'd be delighted to—if I got a pass. I felt happier than I had in a very long time. Someone was showing interest in me for something I loved. Leigh was helping to make it happen. Before we left, Ruth insisted we try her lasagna and antipasto salad. Used to hospital food, we wolfed it down. Done, we reluctantly said goodbye, the scent of eucalyptus clinging to our clothes. I associated that smell with Zili's house, the first person who taught me to understand the life-giving power of art. I had never forgotten that vow.

The following day, I asked Archibald for a pass to visit the Pintos, explaining how important this was. He insisted I'd find greater emotional stability if I gave up unrealistic fantasies of being an artist. If my plans didn't work out, I'd set myself up for depression.

I asked, "And if they *do* work out?" I presented my case—no cutting, no incidents. He stressed I shouldn't get swept up by expectations. I said I understood. *Placate, placate.* He wanted to see me after I returned. I thanked him and asked another favor: to come to O.T., to see the work I'd been creating for the Pintos. Even though I doubted he'd come, I needed him to understand I was willing to work hard. He looked me in the eyes and said he'd try.

As I headed out front, to see the coral-colored azaleas, I spotted Peggy. She said, "Where's your purple hat the hat you wore the night when faces cracked inside walls?"

Her comment convinced me to wear my purple top hat to visit Ruth. I told Peggy a woman might help me get out of the Toot. I felt in my gut something was changing.

"Purple hat purple hat," Peggy laughed, unable to keep talking. She didn't even respond when I said I loved her and always would.

In the intervening week, I told only Chambliss and Terri about my appointment. I swore them to secrecy— didn't want to jinx it. Terri was thrilled. Chambliss, less so. Maybe she was starting to think she'd never get out—a fear we all shared. Leigh knew I was seeing Ruth, but I never worried about her telling anyone; she had little contact with the patients. She continued to see the Toot as a joke, her stay there as a convenience for her mother and uncle. She told me she'd be out in a few weeks. Meanwhile, she comforted herself with an imaginary life as exotic as the Gauguin posters covering her walls. Those walls, that room had once been Lenore's.

I funneled my energy into making artwork every available day at O.T.—arriving early, staying late. I wanted to impress the Pintos. It was my chance to finally get confirmation that the part of me that had been treated like a disease was actually healthy and beautiful.

The excursion day came. The bus let me off on Twenty-Second and Market. I hiked to Delancey Street. Cradling my portfolio, I was carrying my future. Suddenly, a woman darted in front of me in a shiny, yellow coat. A man stepped out of a yellow cab, carrying yellow bags. A lemon-colored ball rolled by; a boy with a yellow 5 on his shirt chased it. It was a color-coordinated day. I never understood them but had had them before. They always meant something good was operating beyond my control, something changing my life.

I arrived at Ruth's townhouse. Up the marble steps, I tapped with the brass knocker. The door swung open. Wearing a clingy, silver jumpsuit with a monk's cowl, Ruth invited me in. She had just made manicotti. The house smelled of garlic, tomato sauce, and eucalyptus leaves.

"Smells good, Mrs. Pinto."

"Please, call me Ruth. Are you hungry?"

"Sure."

"There's nothing like home-cooked food, *n'est-ce pas*?"

Afraid of sounding ignorant, I didn't ask what *n'est-ce pas* meant. I soon learned it was one of her favorite phrases.

"When you marry Italian, you learn to cook like one," she said.

I laughed nervously.

"English-German stock myself, but I can cook like a Neapolitan." She asked me to serve myself and take my plate to the den. She carried hers to a rococo desk with a wicker swing hanging behind it. As she balanced on the swing, she matter-of-factly pointed to a Chinese chair, saying that every night when she meditated, the spirit of her guru sat there. Afraid of squashing him, I sat on the leather couch, beneath a clown—one of her husband's paintings.

"Reminds me of Soutine and Rouault," I said.

She said her husband loved Soutine. She saw the Rouault influence, too.

"The black lines," I said, adding I had studied art since I was a kid.

"So, you think you're a genius?"

"Why, did I say something egotistical?" *Have I messed this up already?*

"Heavens, no. The world will knock you down if you don't believe in yourself."

It was a very different message from the one I'd received from Archibald and my father. "Well, look at my work first."

She called out to her husband, reminding him I was there. He shuffled into the room in leather slippers, wearing glasses so thick his dark eyes swam behind them like carp. He introduced himself and joked about artists having no sense of time, making me feel at ease right away. Asking me to open my portfolio on the coffee table, they looked intently as I turned the paintings, drawings, and prints.

He said, "Dean has a fine sense of line. Suggests volume."

They were both impressed by a picture of dancing women with full skirts, which I had drawn with markers on paper toweling. The swirling hems implied movement. Ruth lifted the drawing gingerly and placed it aside. I explained, without feeling foolish, that I'd heard music in my head as I drew the picture. The magenta, carmine, and yellow skirts whirled to the melodies—a transcription of sound. Ruth and her husband understood what I meant. Sure, my ideas made sense to me, but I could never share them with Dad or Archibald, for fear of being labeled "euphoric" or worse.

With each piece the Pintos scrutinized, I felt closer to being appreciated. They admired a pen-and-ink drawing of a holly sprig, saying it reminded them of Japanese woodblock prints. I told them I'd loved Japanese art since Mom had given me a book on Harunobu. Ruth and her husband selected more pieces than I thought they would for the "yes" pile, to prove my talent.

"Dean, you're a little master," her husband proclaimed, looking at a slide of an oil painting I'd done years before. I said I'd created that at ten, reliving the day: Our art teacher had us do paintings of old farm houses. I had just come back to art class after Mom's hospitalization—in the same facility where I ended up.

Even though I hadn't smoked pot, I felt as if I'd taken a pill that dissolves inhibitions. I described seeing blue air between branches and trying to paint it. I asked if that made sense, scared of sounding like a crazy kid from a nut house. Her husband said that was negative space, which he'd struggled to convey to his students. Emboldened, I admitted that if I looked hard, I could see colors inside colors. He added that anyone who mixes paints knows that. The Pintos spoke my language and believed there was something of worth in me. Scared they'd think I was a fraud later on, I wouldn't allow myself to give in to that fear.

Unexpectedly, a girl my age darted into the kitchen—their daughter. She stole a glimpse of me from around the wall. To dispel her bashfulness, Ruth said I was a nice artistic kid. The girl padded into the den, said "Hi," and scampered off with a plate of manicotti and salad.

Ruth explained her daughter was not only painfully shy, but she was barely making it in school. "You gifted kids have a rough time." Shifting her tone, she asked how long I'd been at the Institute. I said I'd been there almost two years and was afraid of never getting out.

Her husband was visibly saddened, which hadn't been my intent. He started going over the "yes" pile again, no longer involved in the conversation, the black carp behind his glasses hovering in place.

Ruth asked if we had a school. I told her about Matthew and the college-level books we read. I said a high point had been going to The Philadelphia Museum of Art and The Barnes Foundation. I was stunned to learn her husband had paintings in their collection. But I wasn't expecting what she said next, "Would you like getting into an arts high school?"

My head swam. Tongue-tied, I managed to say it would be the most amazing thing in the world—as long as it wasn't a boarding school. Assuring me it would be in Philadelphia, she asked why I made that distinction. I told her I'd been sent to one and how kids had ganged together to steal my things, destroy my homework, and shove me down a flight of stairs. I was afraid of being killed. She shook her head, saying nothing surprised her, asking if an adult had spoken out. No one with power, I said. To the contrary, staff members insisted I toughen up.

She said her daughter's life had been hellish, too. The kids, the teachers all let her know she didn't belong. That inspired Ruth to create a school for talented kids, certain there was a pattern to the abuse we experienced. "People need scapegoats, and if kids are different. . . ." Then, as if finding the words for a mission statement, she said, "Imagine feeling a part *of*, not apart *from*." Her unblinking eyes encompassed me.

Breaking the spell, her husband asked where my parents lived. I explained that after the divorce, Mom had moved to Philly, near the art museum. Dad stayed in South Jersey.

"Maybe I could invite them over," Ruth said.

My breath leapt in my chest. I couldn't stop feeling excited. "O-of course," I said.

She did soon meet with my parents, individually, talking to them about her school. Having been working out the details for at least a year, her ideas were cogent enough to convince them and benefactors. Within a month, a board of directors had a meeting. What shocked me most—she had invited my parents and Archibald to attend. They all agreed to go.

After that meeting, he and I had a session. He seemed to have acquired a new respect for me, no longer observing me as a mentally ill specimen—the way I'd gawked at medical deformities at the Mütter Museum. Leigh and I had gone there on an outing. The more gruesome the specimens, the more we liked them. They were "oddities," like us. A lit cabinet showcased the infant skeletons of dwarfs. But the most disturbing thing was the face in a jar—not because it was ghoulish, but because it was sad.

Sliced neatly from its head, it was the shape and color of a pear. Suspended in formaldehyde by two spokes, it had a mournful expression. Its eyes looked down in perpetual regret, its lips parted as if to say, "It would be. . . ."

Those words began Archibald's statement when I saw him the following week, "It would be too early to say conclusively, but I've met with Mrs. Pinto and think highly of her project."

"I'm happy when I visit her."

"She tells me you've been studying meditation, and you're not doing drugs."

"She said meditation doesn't work with drugs." She had taught me to repeat the sacred sound *Om* as a mantra. Closing my eyes, breathing it in and out, I imagined riding through the waves of my emotions, holding onto a turquoise dolphin.

"It seems the Pintos are having a positive effect." He followed by saying he needed to make sure it wasn't just a phase.

Typical doubletalk, but tell him whatever he wants to hear. "That makes perfect sense," I lied. I wouldn't let him prevent me from going to her school. I'd do whatever it took.

CHAPTER 28
A PART, NOT APART

While Terri never managed to win over Boxer, I kept my own feelings toward him hidden. Besides, he was no longer the boy we knew. Nurses drugged him with stronger antipsychotic medications to subdue his increasingly violent behavior. I worried he'd get a lobotomy, like Peggy.

Once, after seeing her, other patients and I talked about that procedure. David described the surgeon shoving something like an ice pick up the patient's eye socket. Jabbing, the doctor mutilated the offending brain matter—source of the violent, antisocial acts.

"Did they know how much brain to destroy?" Chambliss asked.

"No," David said. That was the problem. As a result, some people who had this barbaric operation simply became flattened versions of their former selves. Others, like Peggy, became eternal children. Still others could no longer dress or feed themselves, needing help to use the toilet. They stared into space, drooling. I would never forgive the Toot if they did that to Boxer. Glasses convinced us lobotomies were no longer performed.

I never saw him again. He was placed on the wing for violent patients. I heard how, for days on end, those patients slobbered in drug-induced stupors, restrained with leather straps, sitting in their own filth. One of the aides said, "Poor boy, he's got dark circles under his eyes. Gained so much weight. You wouldn't recognize him."

He was the first man I ever fell in love with.

We never heard anything more about Lenore and stopped asking for our own emotional survival. We expected she'd continue to hear the hellish voices, instructing her to slash deeper, and finally, nurses wouldn't get there in time, or they might just be too busy playing bridge to care. Cora told us—because she had worked at that facility—murders had taken place. Women (and men) were raped and killed. One patient had been partially eaten.

Given my closeness to Cora, I finally asked her why, when she came from the Philippines, she couldn't find a nicer job.

"Like what? A maid?"

"At least it wouldn't be so depressing," I said.

"Dino, the good Lord directed me here." She told me her sister had been in a mental hospital. Unable to afford one as nice as the Toot, she was put in a state institution. Like Lenore, her sister heard terrible voices in her head. The orderlies found her hanging from a noose made of shredded clothes and declared it a suicide. "I'll never believe it," Cora said.

Her profound compassion came from understanding a tortured mind, an understanding Archibald seemed to lack. "So why not work at a state hospital? They might need you," I said.

"I wouldn't last in one of those places."

I understood her pain and regret. Our compassion ran both ways. Hers had helped me hold onto the belief that I'd someday get free.

While participating in scheduled events, I felt like

I was floating through the motions. Sure, Glasses still conducted Morning Meetings. The jerk in Group continued to fling insults. But I began to picture a life for myself outside the wall—*a part of, not apart from.*

It was already happening. Thanks to the Pintos, I started to take drawing classes at the Pennsylvania Academy of the Fine Arts. An open pass allowed me to go back and forth by myself. I loved the smells and atmosphere of such a magnificent art college—like a house of worship. During a break from sketching, I sat on the steps beneath the pointed arch, a notepad on my lap. I tried to describe the images flashing through my head as I drew. As I scribbled the first draft of a poem, I worried if it made sense. Worse yet, it might make me seem crazy. I thought I'd always be branded that way by people "on the outside." Keeping it factual, I wrote about living in an apartment: no need to have someone unlock the door, to get permissions or privileges. That going outside and enjoying life constituted a "privilege" seemed especially cruel. I returned to the class with a renewed conviction that I *would* live in the world like a normal person.

The following day, Leigh and I shared our fantasies of what we'd be doing when we got out. She told me she'd have her own gallery in New York City. Her mother had already made plans for her to intern at one in Philadelphia, after her release. "In five years," Leigh said, "I'll have a chain of galleries across Europe and the States."

I pictured myself painting and writing poems all day, getting paid to do so by wealthy benefactors. Our fantasies had an unbridled sense of possibility. If we wanted something, we could make it happen. Our lack of realism came from having been sequestered too long, like overgrown bulbs, locked away and forgotten in a root cellar. But the quality of our imaginings also sprang up in revolt to the tyranny of limitation. We needed to affirm its opposite, the way a poor person dreams of having a private jet and chauffeur, not simply the essentials of a middle-class life. Our audacious daydreams sustained us.

I never understood why Leigh was in the Toot in the first place. I doubted *she* did. I guessed her mother found it expedient—having her hands too full with Uncle, not to mention her own unacknowledged alcoholism.

Leigh and I got another pass together and explored the antique district. She loved vintage clothes and—when she wasn't wearing hand-painted skirts—dressed like Madame Bovary without the corsets. Old things, like old movies, gave us a sense of continuity, of survival. A window display featured laces draped over old furniture. Entering the store, we eyed shelves of jewelry. Mother's Day was coming up, and I needed to buy a present. I asked to look at a Victorian brooch: A filigree spider clung to a web, a dewdrop on its back. Because a spider builds webs all alone, it seemed like an emblem of self-sufficiency. Divorced, Mom would be independent. Even if she didn't get the intended symbolism, she'd appreciate the pin's beauty. I bought it with all the spending money I had left.

Leigh pointed to a grandfather clock: time to go back to the Toot. It was an unusually cold April. Winds and icy rains bit into us as we left the store. With bent umbrellas, we traipsed to the bus. As we rode back, rain streamed down the windows, infused with lights from passing cars. Lit with a red glow, Leigh's face exposed something I hadn't seen before: fear. I reminded her she'd have her chain of galleries, and the two of us were close to getting released. I said it to cheer her up, but I really believed it about myself.

After all, Ruth was on my side. Her charismatic ability to persuade people seemed both heroic and magical. She'd been meeting with benefactors who would help her to establish the high school for gifted kids. Even skeptics came around to supporting her. One of them was my father. He might have enjoyed a painting because it made him feel good, but not for its artistic merit. He'd written books on law and read about history and politics, but never novels or poetry. Nonetheless, he became one of Ruth's most ardent supporters in her quest to establish the school. He even came up with its name: The Seminar of Arts and Sciences. Ruth had wielded some benevolent magic, transforming him into someone who cared about art.

In time, he tried to see many things from my perspective, taking an interest in the books and Beatles' songs I loved. Having grasped the severity of my depression, and how his treating me as "sickening" had contributed to it, he tried to make amends. Despite my distrust of him—which I'd worn like armor—I had to acknowledge his effort. Ruth had been helping me in that regard. "To *re-sent* means to *re-feel*," she said. "When you resent someone, you keep feeling the hurt." Visiting her, I began to question my encrusted anger.

Her house, alive with art, cooking, and even her

fashion designs, was always open to me. One day when I dropped by, she was preparing for company, so I helped by washing dishes and cutting loaves of bread. Because we were alone, I found the courage to ask how she'd gotten interested in Vedanta (the ancient Indian philosophy based on the Vedas) and sculpture. I needed to understand how I could change.

She told me she was from Ohio. Her parents also divorced. Like me, she found herself given to long periods of depression. After moving to New York City, to pursue a career in acting, she started to run with a group of wild friends. As a prank, they'd written a girl's name and phone number on the wall of a men's bathroom. Some sadist called the girl, got her address, raped, and murdered her. Ruth was devastated. She lost all interest in her friends and acting. An acquaintance told her about the Rosicrucian Order. She was sure it could turn her life around, but the headquarters were in California. With almost no money, she hitchhiked. The Rosicrucianists disappointed her too. Someone had bludgeoned a devotee—all evidence concealed from the police.

Convinced nothing in life could go right, Ruth hitchhiked again, this time to a cliff above the Pacific: Point Dume, famous for suicides. (Here was our bond and I hadn't realized it.) Instead, the driver took her to the Vedanta Temple in Hollywood. He never divulged his affiliation, and she knew nothing about this religion. The stranger said he'd wait in his car for an hour. If she came out, he'd drive her to the precipice.

He waited. She stayed inside.

She went on to live as a nun for three years. Every

Sunday, the sisters drove from Santa Barbara to the Los Angeles ashram, where she met Christopher Isherwood and Aldous Huxley. Nervous about meeting the famous men, she found them approachable.

She confided having witnessed incredible feats: Her guru summoned a jacaranda tree to bend down and brush his outstretched hand. Yogis levitated in meditation. She made these statements with such conviction that I believed a holy person could do anything—like the saints my grandmother had told me about.

But I still wanted to know how Ruth had become a sculptor. Her guru worshipped Kali, the goddess of destruction, her torso draped in a necklace of skulls. I was visibly horrified. Destruction, Ruth explained, is as necessary for birth as winter is for spring. Her guru and his followers celebrated Kali's holy day by renting a helicopter and dropping a life-sized sculpture of the deity into the Pacific, where Ruth had considered leaping. The guru chose her to make the sculpture, convincing her that Kali would guide her hands. Although she had never sculpted before, she molded the figure with virtuosity. The goddess seemed to erupt from the clay.

Five male devotees hauled the sculpture into a helicopter, chanting. Intoning a Sanskrit mantra, they released the statue from the hatch. I pictured Kali splitting the water, her four arms slicing the waves, driving her weight down. I imagined veils sprouting from her shoulders as she danced, her necklace of skulls flickering.

Seeing how spellbound I was, Ruth hugged me and said, "We've got work to do."

We prepared the living room in time for the arrival of guests. Before changing into a white jumpsuit with a monk's cowl, she told me to help myself to some Indian food in the kitchen. I sat at the counter and put my plate on the white Formica. Her daughter had covered the surface with masterful pencil drawings of ocelots, ancient Egyptians, and alien spacecraft coexisting in some other dimension.

As people arrived and gathered in the den, I listened to their conversations. Ruth held court, enthroned on the persimmon chair. Detailing her vision of a school for artistically talented teens, she asked, "Can you imagine a place where these kids can feel *a part of, not apart from*?"

That had become my mantra.

The doorbell rang. Ruth greeted the guest with a bright, "Oh hi, Hank. So glad you could make it!" I had no idea who "Hank" was until they passed the kitchen where I sat eating chickpea curry. He was Dr. Archibald. I went red-faced, seeing him in my new sanctuary, where he seemed less sinister. He smiled toothily and joined the adults.

As much as I wanted to eavesdrop on their conversation, I had to get back for class. But before leaving, I overheard her showing various kids' artwork, to prove her position. Mine was the third group. Based on the *oh*'s and complimentary things people said, they were impressed. I could have listened to that all day. Beaming, I washed my plate, tiptoed into the den, telling Ruth and Archibald I'd see them soon.

CHAPTER 29
BIRTHDAY

Matthew had us perform Chekhov's *The Seagull*. I chose the role of Konstantin. He and I even have the same name, Dean coming from *Konstandinos*. The play about a despondent young man would have been impossible for me to read six months earlier. By the final act, the room fell into a hush of collective empathy for my character. He shot himself—a fantasy I'd contemplated. My eyes welled up, but I didn't mind Matthew seeing. He was the one who'd rescued me after my last suicide attempt. And even though the idea of shooting myself no longer gripped me, the urge to take my life hadn't disappeared. Its shadowy vestige hovered in the back of my mind, with one major difference: I had power over *it*.

Things of greater importance inflamed my thoughts. I was one month shy of sixteen, obsessed with how kids lived in the world. They seemed as fictitious as Konstantin. But instead of thinking about a nineteenth-century character, I craved the contemporary trends of young people. I needed to see what they were wearing and how they were dancing. The music they listened to played all day on our turntables. Those songs had become our lifeline to the outside, a world I'd given up being a part of.

But that was changing. For the first time in nearly two years, people with authority over my life acted more like friends than adversaries. Ruth's influence on Archibald had shifted his perception of me. He apologized for having discouraged my dedication to painting. That marked a fundamental change, a border crossed.

I knew then art would be the thing to get me out of the Toot. I knew then I would enjoy a life beyond its stone wall, breathing freedom's air. I knew then where Ruth's "Seminar" would lead me—that I'd spend my last two years of high school there, graduating from it. I knew then I would paint myself to sanity—that I'd feel whole, my brushstrokes twisting into poems. I knew then art would guide me: the credo sworn years before with a noose around my neck.

At Ruth's house, I rediscovered awe. Although visions of patients' grotesque and desperate acts had filled my eyes, all that hurt and terror seemed to dissipate. In her presence, I found my way back to the wonder I'd known as a boy, but with a variation. As a child, with my easel and palette, I needed to understand the colors inside colors. I needed to grasp what I couldn't see. Ruth loaned me books on mysticism. I learned about Indian sages and their teachings. While the Sanskrit words and ideas were sometimes confusing, I devoured the texts like nourishment.

That God hated me for being attracted to men, and would punish me with eternal damnation, tainted my relationship to Christianity. Vedanta was as far away from the religion of my childhood as I could get. Or so I thought. Through my studies with Ruth I came back to my affection for the Good Shepherd prayed to at my grandmother's altar. But with new eyes. I learned that Sri Ramakrishna, a nineteenth-century mystic, had had ecstatic visions of Jesus. I also learned that Hindus can worship God as a romantic partner. Tortured by my erotic fantasies of the crucified Savior, I needed to no longer feel like a "sinner," to stop hating myself. From a Hindu perspective, I realized my desires may have been an attempt to see Christ as the Beloved. Maybe I wasn't evil after all. Ruth also guided me to read books on western mysticism, pointing to saints who had worshipped the Lord as spouse. The idiosyncratic ideas I developed from reading those books led me to erase the differences between Christianity and Hinduism. While some people would find my blending these religions illogical or offensive, it affirmed a new way of being no one could ever take from me.

As much as I cherished my visits to Ruth's house, she was always mindful of my schedule at the Toot. She said I had to follow their rules if I wanted to get released and join her school. Looking at her watch, she reminded me I had therapy. I hugged her, closed the door behind me, and headed to the Toot.

In my visit with "Hank," I looked out the window. It was late April and the gardeners were working on the grounds, planting more coral, yellow, and white azaleas. Color spoke to me so deeply I could never find words to equal it. Archibald thought I was ignoring him. Getting my attention, he conveyed how impressed he was with Ruth and her ideas, saying, "She and her husband think you're quite gifted."

"Gifted?" I could hear that word forever.

"I've done you an injustice," he said.

I looked him straight in the eyes, unable to believe he'd spoken those words. "Thanks, I guess."

"Well, don't thank me yet," he said. "We've been observing your behavior over the last six months. We're amazed at how changed you seem to be." He was signing papers on his desk, throwing others into the dented trash can. "No," he corrected himself, "how changed you *are*."

"It's the meditation," I said.

And then he said something that shocked me, "I'm planning to visit the Ramakrishna monastery."

"In India?" I asked.

"Yes, to research the effects of meditation on brainwaves."

"Didn't think this stuff would interest you."

"I studied Ancient Greek philosophy, and some Hindu tenets are similar to Plato's."

"I'm surprised."

"Well, I'm full of surprises," he said.

"Such as?"

"Some *very* good news." He stopped sorting the papers. Looking at me, he said, "You're getting out. It's final."

I felt dizzy, couldn't catch my breath. "When?"

"Next month, mostly for administrative details. We do a lot of dotting and crossing here."

"You have a date?"

"May twenty-first."

"My birthday?" Head spinning, I stuttered, "Th ... thank you."

I didn't know whom to tell first. I considered not telling patients who might not be getting out soon. I ran to share the news with Cora, who squeezed me. I dashed to O.T., telling every friend, starting with Leigh. She'd been the conduit, after all. Everyone was thrilled and said they'd miss me. Some went silent. I knew why.

I spotted Peggy on the lawn. She'd noticed the new azaleas. "Peggy, I have really great news. I'm getting out in a month—for good. I'll get to do fun things like normal kids."

She tore out pictures of people from the newspaper and then cut off their heads. Humming to herself, she didn't look up. Her new red wig had straight bangs like a doll's. Unsure if she'd heard me, I said, "I'll visit you, Peggy, I promise. But I'll be free. Please be happy for me."

"The rain is here car lights shoot colors through my window watery flowers a see-through garden."

"Beautiful, Peggy. I'll always remember you."

I spent every day from that point on, imagining my release. The month passed more quickly and more slowly than I thought it would. Then Cora told me my parents had arrived. Mom burst into my room with a ringing, "Dino!" My father followed behind her. They'd come in separate cars, but entered the room together. They smelled fresh, carrying the scent of freedom.

The rain Peggy described sluiced down my window. My record albums, books, O.T. projects, posters, and clothes were all packed in crates and suitcases, wrapped in layers of plastic drop cloths. My white room was as stark as exposed bone. I darted through halls, the gym, the grounds—hugging as many of my friends as I ran into.

Dad, meanwhile, started loading the trunks of both cars. Phil—seen only on excursions—had come to help. The cars were packed.

Cora, Matthew, Terri, Chambliss, Leigh, David, Lion Boy, and three aides all held black umbrellas, escorting me in what looked like a religious procession. With even steps, they led me to Mom's car, rain tinging on its roof. I held each one of my friends, wishing I could take them with me. I was drenched but didn't care. Neither did they. I paused and looked at Cora and Matthew. Leaning forward to embrace them, I said, "You've helped me more than anyone. How can I ever thank you?"

"Dean, we've gotta get going," Mom said and then mouthed, *Sorry.* She pushed the electric button, closing the windows with a purr, her face replaced by reflections.

I pulled myself away from Cora, Matthew, and my friends, sliding into the seat. I waved through the glass, jawing, *Good-bye.* I waved until I could no longer see them.

Until the wall concealed them.

Until the wall disappeared.

Epilogue

"You've gotta be kidding!" That's what friends say when I tell them I was a suicidal fourteen-year-old who spent two years in a mental hospital. Today, they know me as someone who's happy, productive, and reasonably well-adjusted.

I remind them, "It was a long time ago. I've had years to work through the pain, trauma, and anger." Friends ask why I tried to take my life. I tell them my family was imploding, I was tormented mercilessly at school, and I saw no other way out. That was long before adults got involved to prevent bullying. Although adolescent suicide has been on the rise for the last fifty years, the attitude until only recently has been, "Toughen up!"

Luckily, I didn't become a statistic, nor was I hospitalized again. I managed that by severing ties with the Toot and seeing no one from that life—agonizing as that choice was. I focused on Ruth's school, from which I graduated at a garden party. But my memory of fellow patients has never left me. They follow me like specters, connecting our past to my present. As Tennessee Williams writes, "Time is the longest distance between two points." I've done my best to reconstruct the patients' hurts, voices, and beautiful audacity.

In order to make peace with my past, I've had to revisit it. To navigate back, I needn't look farther than the underside of my left arm: a constellation of seven moon-shaped scars. Now, the act of cutting myself is so alien, it seems as if someone else made those marks.

My journey toward wholeness has been slow. I came out at eighteen, having the courage to do so after seeing Christopher Isherwood on TV. He unapologetically declared himself gay. I first told my father and then my mother. He said, "I've always known, but I used to think in black-and-white. Now, I've come to see life in tonalities of gray. If you're happy, that's all I care about." I was astonished. It showed how much we'd grown together. Sadly, Mom blamed herself, as mothers are taught to do when a son is gay. Unable to get out bed for a week, she slept and cried, going back on sedatives. Eventually, she rallied and accepted me.

When I was twenty, she and I visited relatives in Greece. I left her in Athens and sailed to Mykonos, where I spent a day in Super Paradise—a clothing-optional beach. (I wore a bathing suit.) Spotting a young woman I'd known briefly at the Toot, I called her name. She stopped with her boyfriend and peered over large sunglasses. Both she and the young man were naked except for gold jewelry, seemingly molten in the Greek sun. Despite the awkward situation, I learned she had changed her name, as if casting off clothes soiled by a crime. We joked about not being in Mykonos on an excursion, but winced instead. She reminded me how lucky we were to get out. Not everyone had been so fortunate. I thought of Lenore with a stab of guilt. The nude woman tugged her boyfriend's hand and headed to a dance club.

Long after Mykonos, through my twenties, I struggled to fight off what I described as "numbing darkness." It appeared from nowhere and clung to almost everything I thought and tried to accomplish like a web of thorns.

It forced me to drop out of college several times and to end friendships. It impeded my ability to understand the past. My stay at the Toot had robbed me of more than a decade, beyond the two years I lived there. Writing this memoir has been an act of reclamation.

But I never could have unearthed that past and cast it into language without having grown a solid self—a foundation to withstand the aftershocks. It's also probably the reason for my migrating from being a visual artist to being a poet. Daubs of paint curled into words.

That's not to say I'll ever be free of my history. The word *crazy* upsets my mother and me more than any insult. It's the one word against which we've measured our thoughts, emotions, and actions. The residual shame of feeling isolated from the world persists.

For that reason, I've researched psychological concepts. The numbing darkness has a clinical name: post-traumatic stress disorder. As I read about it, it made perfect sense, yet no therapists had identified it. Psychologists originally recognized PTSD in military personnel, but recent studies show the syndrome can affect anyone. On the word of psychologist Laurence Miller, "Witnessing violent acts or horrifying events" can trigger it. In addition to recognizing the "psychological numbing and avoidance" that go along with PTSD, Miller writes that it often causes one to "feel estranged from other people, and the world appears hostile, remote, or changed." *Estranged, hostile, remote, changed.* Those words sum up the states I battled for more than a decade after my release.

Healing has come in many guises. Therapy has

helped, as have my quirky sense of humor and my love of art, but only in addition to practices begun years ago in Ruth's house. Today, in my bedroom, an icon of Jesus (blessed by Swami Prabhavananda) stands among figurines of Krishna, Shiva, and Archangel Michael. Kriya breathing exercises, prayer, and meditation have healed my depressions more than years of therapy.

I've also made peace with Dr. Archibald. Even though he infuriated me, I had no way of knowing his remarks were unprofessional—a form of sexual abuse. That's what I believe; I have no way to prove it. As a teen, I ascribed wisdom to adults, respecting what they said and did. It wasn't until I started writing this memoir, reconstructing conversations, that I heard his comments more clearly. Back then, I thought they were "therapeutic," meant to enrage me. To be sure, I had trouble showing anger, having grown up in a school and home where to do so was dangerous. But in the process of peeling back memories, I heard his tone, saw his lewd gaze and body language, with one distinction—I'm an adult. If a therapist said similar things to me today, I'd fire him. Better yet, I'd report him. I've made room for my wrath and have finally come to compassion. In his generation, he couldn't have risen to the top of his profession as a single man, let alone as an openly gay one. His colleagues labeled homosexuality a "mental disorder." But sexuality is untidy. If you suppress it, it pounces back when least expected. I assume Dr. Archibald lived in the closet, but living such a lie is a dank prison. It not only affects the life of the closeted person—it infects the family, colleagues, and patients—as I blatantly experienced. I was his self-hatred (disguised as desire). He was mine (disguised as fear).

It was a different time; no one talked about sexual identity. I'd like to believe LGBTQ kids today get the support I never had. But things haven't changed enough. Teen suicide rages on as an epidemic. The Internet posts face after face of the victims. Like vapor, they vanish from our consciousness. I see myself in each boy and girl. Whenever possible, I've reached out to ostracized youths in my capacity as a professor.

Years ago, I worked as a "teaching artist," introducing poetry writing to ninth graders (the age I was when hospitalized). It was the same high school my mother had attended. When I worked there, however, it was plagued by violence: Police patrolled hallways. Kids stabbed other kids in stairwells. I relived my adolescent dread. As an adult, I was protected. Had anyone attacked me, he would've been expelled. Students weren't so lucky. A boy in my class carried photographs of oiled wrestlers. After finishing my assignments, he'd open the centerfolds to show me. Other boys said, "Why the fuck you carryin' around pictures of naked men?"

"They're wrestlers," he shot back. His poems detailed beatings he'd received.

I couldn't bring myself to say, *I'm gay too, and kids picked on me. I'll protect you.* I was afraid of losing my job, of seeming "predatory." I couldn't say, *I've seen you in the hallway, your shoulders hunched to ward off attacks. Shame has started to deform you.* All I could say was, "Just think, in three years you'll be out of here—an adult." I can only hope he's gone on to flourish, free of his past.

I needed to do the same. One of the blessings of adulthood is the horizontal gaze achieved with parents. I wanted to understand what led to Mom's nervous breakdown. For my commencement ceremony from grad school, she flew with me to Ohio. We arrived at Dayton and stayed at a hotel. We had dinner at its restaurant, which transformed into a cabaret. A singer crooned Sinatra songs, the melancholy lilt of his voice infusing the room. Perhaps it was the music or the unfamiliar city, but Mom and I talked more freely than we ever had. As I came to learn of her affairs, I felt neither judgment nor anger. With my own failed relationships, I've become pragmatic: Human beings are like plants, leaning toward any available light. My mother had fallen in love with the owner of a car dealership. He'd meet her in a blazer with slicked-back hair, drive her to a restaurant, and hold her hand. She'd unburden herself, divulging her struggles and aspirations. I picture their bodies moving in unison, a water ballet. She always returned before school let out, there when my brother and I got home.

Guilt-ridden, she broke off the affair. But the man's love for her refused to die. He drove to our house, waiting to convince her that she needed him, too. Instead, he glimpsed her closest female friend. He waved his arms, calling out to her. This usually well-groomed man stood there, tie undone, blazer wrinkled, hair hanging in his eyes, sobbing. He begged her to listen. Before she drove away, he threw himself onto the hood of her car, pounding, "Tell Sofia I need her!" Her friend conveyed his message, but Mom wouldn't budge: The affair was over.

She tried to forget him by studying political science in Philadelphia. Wanting to discuss world events with Dad, to be treated as his peer, she drove thirty miles each way to a Monday-night course. She'd ask her handsome professor questions after class, staying five minutes, then fifteen. Going out for coffee, she found herself in his arms, kissing. They had long philosophical discussions, which she never had with my father. However, when the course ended, she said their affair had to stop. She had two little boys; it wasn't right. But nothing could quash the fear that she'd thrown away her only chance for happiness. She had to deaden the pain.

Doing chores, she drove to the drycleaner's, chatting with the owner. He noticed she was upset and convinced her he was a certified psychologist *and* a licensed hypnotist. Joking about cleaning more than just clothes, he could scour agonizing memories. Naïve, she underwent hypnosis. While it dislodged the pangs of loss, it unleashed repressed memories of her father's death and sister's beatings. That led to Mom's nervous breakdown.

Her sharing these incidents was a gift. Understanding her past engendered respect for the powerful, creative, and decent person she is. She's gone on to become a sculptor, award-winning photographer, genocide-awareness activist, and a fervent supporter of LGBTQ rights. I'd like to think I've inherited even half of her dynamism.

While my mother and I have communicated openly, other people depicted in this memoir may claim I've gotten the details wrong. The best I can do is to write *my* emotional truth, none of it governed by malice.

And yes, some people I have written about are easier to love than others.

My grandmother is one of these. Visiting her for Saturday lunches, I napped afterward in her small guest room, to soak in the feeling of safety. As I lay on her small bed, she covered me with a blanket, a tarnished bas-relief of the Virgin Mary gazing down from the wall.

Years later, my mother, stepfather, and I visited my grandmother for Thanksgiving. She was bedridden, so we spoon-fed her broth and juice. During the five minutes we spent in the other room, she died at the age of 103. Because of the holiday, undertakers were slow to arrive. The three of us took turns, sitting vigil with her body. I watched her face change—her corpse preparing itself for release. The process felt neither gruesome nor disturbing, but was a final act of love.

As for Dad, making peace with him was curtailed by his Parkinson's disease. To purge our troubled history, I took the bus every month from New York to Philadelphia, suctioning his tracheotomy for hours. This eloquent man was stripped, little-by-little, of movement, sight, speech. As he received larger doses of Levadopa, he suffered temporary periods of psychosis, hallucinating insects with his parents' faces.

Before completely losing his ability to talk, he told me his body had become a prison. In "Elegy for a Living Man," which he never read, I wrote, "From his tracheotomy-hole, / an iridescent weave of lightning // rushed up in the form of a dancer … coaxing him: *Let me go*." The poem appeared in *Boulevard* and later in my chapbook *Celestial Rust*. I never got to share my publications with him.

During one of my visits, his caretaker went out to perform errands. I remained alone with my father. He needed to go to the bathroom. Even though he'd lost many pounds, his body felt like dead weight. It took me forty minutes to carry him to the toilet and to bring him back to his easy chair. I couldn't hold him up. He fell from my arms. Hair tousled, eyes dazed, he resembled an unstrung marionette. But instead of showing him empathy, all the rage I didn't realize I still harbored funneled out like some demonic tornado. I roared, "Why do you always make everything so goddamn impossible?" Even though I regret having said those words, his response was a blessing, as much as Mom's admissions had been. In the best words he could muster, he mumbled, "I never … meant … to hurt … you." In that instant, decades of anger dissolved.

For the last five years of his life, he could no longer eat. Liquid nutrition, called Jevity, was pumped through a hole into his stomach. Eventually, the doctors ran out of alternatives. Solution: Dad spent his final days in a hospice at Graduate Hospital, receiving *nothing* but morphine. The specialist said he'd last a few days. Instead, he went on—in fetal position, his skin granite-gray—for nearly three weeks. I sat by his side for hours, as he had sat with me when I went through detoxification. In the silence, I'd slip from the room to sob, splash my face with cold water, and return. The first line of Sylvia Plath's poem, "The Moon and the Yew Tree," repeated like an icy mantra: "This is the light of the mind, cold and planetary."

I thought, *I'll smother him with a pillow, ending this cruelty. No one will find out.* I fought the temptation, realizing my act of mercy could land me in prison. When he died three weeks later, I was grateful for our reconciliation. Contrary to his fear that no one would attend his funeral, the church was packed. The obituary informed me he had written several books on law.

I now have my own health challenge, a chronic liver disease I contracted from needles shared with Al at the Toot. Hepatitis C is a blood-borne illness, needles the primary means of transmission. As a man, I find myself threatened by a potentially fatal virus given to me by a boy who saw his life as worthless.

I tried the interferon-ribavirin protocol, but abandoned it after two months. Among eighteen intolerable side effects, it brought on a clinical depression more truculent than any I experienced as a teen. I continued taking the New York City subways to work. Overcome by an urge to throw myself before oncoming trains, I clung to girders. At work, I escaped into the men's room to sob, as I had for my father. But, brought on by a chemically induced depression, these tears weren't cathartic. When I got home, I closed my eyes and saw black glass gnashing like teeth, as I had in adolescence.

Finally, when the slightest tap on my hand caused severe bruising, I learned my platelets were dangerously low and that I had to stop the injections immediately. I abandoned the "protocol" and have chosen, contrary to doctors' wishes, to take herbal supplements. To this day, my liver function remains normal.

My adolescent self would have been surprised to learn that the older man he's become has fought so desperately to live. I imagine running after my young self, to let him learn he'll prevail, that *I* will be his father, but I never catch up. Perhaps he's wise, knowing I can only exist in the present.

I now live in the apartment where my mother grew up—where her sister beat her; where my grandmother offered shelter to countless homeless women.

The guest room where my grandmother slept, where I napped, is my office. It's where I grade papers and prepare lessons for classes I teach at The City University of New York and at Columbia. When asked to create a writing-intensive for CUNY, I constructed Literature and Mental Illness. A play we examined through the lens of psychology was *The Glass Menagerie*. Williams described it as a "memory play." While students related to siblings struggling against a controlling mother, they didn't always comprehend her motivation: to make sure her afflicted children would survive without her. The playwright introduces us to three damaged characters, inviting us to find compassion for each one.

I ask the reader to offer the same largesse toward the characters in this memoir, even Alton. As years have passed, my anger toward him has softened into pity. To a greater degree than I ever thought possible, my rage toward the bullies, and toward adults who did nothing to protect me from them, has also softened. Although it may never disappear, I feel vindicated. Just recently, an online search revealed Cinnaminson High School's website. It lists an anti-bullying initiative and a Gay and Straight Alliance—both programs unthinkable when I attended that school.

To be fair, I had positive memories there. In an advanced English class, I first fell in love with poetry through Hopkins's "Spring and Fall." My teacher was the first to awaken the possibility that I would someday be a writer.

In fact, below my grandmother's tarnished bas-relief of the Virgin Mary, I've written hundreds of poems, translations, literary critiques, eight books, a choral text, and a play.

I now live where she dwelled for seventy years. As I sit at my computer, her embroidered affirmation— intertwined with anemones—blooms above me.

Her top-floor apartment accommodates my life. I imagine the roof peeled back as I perch above its beams. Looking down on the rooms of past and present, I see both *almost* clearly.

Thank You

It is with gratitude that I list the generous people who contributed $50.00 or more to my Indiegogo campaign. The bigheartedness of those listed below made it possible for me not to teach for an entire semester, thereby allowing me to funnel time and energy into writing and rewriting this memoir:

Patricia Bates
Sevasti Boutos
Philip F. Clark
Jacqueline de Weever
Emily Durso
Fatimah Elsayed
Davidson Garrett
Gwenn Nusbaum
Carl Rosenstock
Beth and Rob Volin

DEAN KOSTOS's most recent collection is *Pierced by Night-Colored Threads*. His previous books include *This Is Not a Skyscraper* (recipient of the Benjamin Saltman Poetry Award, selected by Mark Doty), *Rivering*, *Last Supper of the Senses*, *The Sentence That Ends with a Comma*, and the chapbook *Celestial Rust*. He coedited *Mama's Boy* (a Lambda Book Award finalist) and edited *Pomegranate Seeds* (its debut reading was held at the United Nations).

His poems and personal essays have appeared in over 300 journals and anthologies, such as *Boulevard*, *Chelsea*, *Cimarron Review*, *The Dos Passos Review*, *Mediterranean Poetry* (Sweden), *New Madrid*, *Memoir Journal*, *Southwest Review*, *Stand Magazine* (UK), *Storyscape Journal*, *Western Humanities Review*, and on Oprah Winfrey's website Oxygen.com. His choral text, *Dialogue: Angel of War, Angel of Peace*, was set to music by James Bassi and performed by Voices of Ascension. His literary criticism has appeared on the Harvard University Press website and elsewhere. A multiple Pushcart-Prize nominee, he served as literary judge for Columbia University's Gold Crown Awards and received a Yaddo fellowship.

He has taught at Wesleyan, The Gallatin School of NYU, and The City University of New York. His poem "Subway Silk" was translated into a film by Jill Clark and screened at Tribeca and at the San Francisco Indiefest. He presented his paper "Schemes and Schemata: Endless Play" and read his poems at Harvard's Mahindra Humanities Center.